PITCH PERFECT

PITCH PERFECT

How to Create a Brand People
Cannot Stop Talking About

SRIMOYI BHATTACHARYA

written with
CHINMAYEE MANJUNATH

PENGUIN
VIKING
An imprint of Penguin Random House

VIKING

USA | Canada | UK | Ireland | Australia
New Zealand | India | South Africa | China | Singapore

Viking is part of the Penguin Random House group of companies
whose addresses can be found at global.penguinrandomhouse.com

Published by Penguin Random House India Pvt. Ltd
4th Floor, Capital Tower 1, MG Road,
Gurugram 122 002, Haryana, India

First published in Viking by Penguin Random House India 2021

10 9 8 7 6 5 4

ISBN 9780670094493

Typeset in Adobe Caslon Pro by Manipal Technologies Limited, Manipal
Printed at Replika Press Pvt. Ltd, India

www.penguin.co.in

This is a legitimate digitally printed version of the book and therefore might not
have certain extra finishing on the cover.

Contents

La Parisienne Who Charmed Us   vii

I Storytelling 101: Building Your DNA and Finding Your Voice

1. You Want to Build a Brand but Where Do You Start?   3
2. Know Your Audience   20
3. What Do Voice and Messaging Mean?   28
4. Getting Your Storytelling Right   40

II The Elevator Pitch: What's the Big Idea?

5. Finding Your Bearings   69
6. What Does PR Actually Mean?   76
7. Introducing Your Brand to the World   84
8. Building Relationships and Getting Pitch Perfect   113
9. Save the Date   139

III Grit: Taking Risks and Getting Granular

10. Ring for Change   157
11. How to Pivot to Create a Better Brand   170
12. What Should You Do if Things Go Wrong?   176

IV Legacy: Consolidating Your Brand and Thinking BIG

13. What Is A Legacy and How Can You Build One?   197
14. How Do You Translate Your DNA playbook into the Zeitgeist? 210

V   The Pitch Perfect Playbook   231

Acknowledgments   287

LA PARISIENNE WHO CHARMED US

It all started with her ditching me. I was looking for a new publicist, being utterly disappointed by the series of agencies I had met who promised 'so' many articles. Srimoyi charmed me by speaking in French, flattering my brand, Hidesign, and me, but mainly because she could think. She listened and then spoke about how we would communicate to the right audience through the right media.

I asked her to join me for dinner during one of my trips to Mumbai; she turned me down! I got back at her by asking Sourabh, then her boyfriend and now her husband, to come to pick her up and of course, the gentleman accepted. That was our first battle and, for once, I won. Sri turned out to be a great ally, complementing our weaknesses with her strengths.

I lived in the boondocks of Auroville—allergic to socializing, a nature lover who wanted to rebel. Srimoyi promised to give Hidesign a face and introduce us to the 'sophisticated' world of Mumbai; to tell our story without apologizing for our small-town Pondicherry roots and our unwillingness to follow the trends of European luxury brands.

A few years later, another great mentor and friend, Yves Carcelle, who was the CEO and chairman of Louis Vuitton, which had just invested in Hidesign, shared something similar with me - 'Nobody can love you if they don't know you.' He made me write a book on our ICON bags, and the origin and values of our brand, to ensure that the whole company spoke the same language and expressed the same attributes.

But it was Sri who first went 'out there', made me give interview after interview, repeating my story of rebelling against the 'monoculture' at Princeton, my hippie and counter-culture days, my reason for being in Auroville and how all of these beliefs influenced Hidesign. And how being original and sustainable can only come from our products being handcrafted.

Sri is not Dilip Kapur. I could always tell she felt our product was not 'sophisticated' enough. In the years I have known her she hardly ever carried Hidesign! But she was a superb champion of ours. She insisted the media must hear our real story. She never encouraged me to bullshit or to follow other Indian companies in inventing a European name or false background. To use PR-speak, we never spun a story.

But this does not mean we didn't have any battles. We did, and they were always polite on her part, and not-so-polite on mine. I was singularly focused on my customers. I always believed that it was at our stores, whether in Mumbai, Hong Kong, Sarajevo, or Pondicherry, that the brand was built. It was here that we had to tell our stories directly to the customer. I argued that great international fashion magazines viewed their primary role as being carriers of international brands to India, while Hidesign's role was to tell its story to India and to the world and hence a conflict of interest: they would always treat us as secondary. Sri defended them; she made me advertise consistently to support them. And she was right. I might be correct in my opinion that their primary focus was international brands, but Hidesign still needed them.

The growth of digital has thrown the channels of communication wide open. When a relatively small brand like Hidesign has over a million social media followers and over 300,000 unique visitors monthly on its website, do we need media and PR agencies? How does a media journal justify its 50,000 subscribers and advertising cost of 10x more than an influencer with 200,000 followers? What role does PR have when we control our social media platforms in-house and influencers reach out to us for collaborations? The answer lies in the story the brand tells, and how it builds it up.

In this book, Sri tells a fascinating story of how Japanese designers brought in a fresh wave with their unique world view and aesthetics in Paris in the 1980s. All original design is a reflection of its cultural milieu. Hidesign started with a uniquely international perspective because I was living in the US and was intensely influenced by the cultural revolution of the late 1960s–70s. (As were Apple, Ben & Jerry's, whose founders also came out of that intense time.) Hidesign has been formed by both the idealistic values of Auroville and the burst of energy from a newly dynamic India finding its place on the international stage. Brands like Hidesign that do not follow European trends have a unique and important story to add to the world.

Some years ago I was invited by the Comité Colbert (the collective body of the leaders of French luxury brands) to talk about Hidesign and its future worldview. From Pascale Mussard of Hermès, Yves Carcelle of Louis Vuitton, Sidney Toledano of Dior, Suzy Menkes of the *New York Times*, they were unanimous — You have nothing important to add to the world if you follow us as we already have many failures struggling to follow the few successes at the top. You must tell your own unique story that adds to the richness of the world's fashion culture.

This is a much more difficult task for brands that must build an original, unbeaten path. Commercially, it is so much easier to copy an already known bag than design an original and make it known to the world. That's the continuing role of Sri and her fellow publicists. We build the brands, we build the product, and we have a story to share. But we are not necessarily equipped to share it with the world.

The publicist, like Sri, who is a thinker, is the ally that works with our marketing team to craft the story and then to find a way in this very crowded and noisy world to make it stand out (even noisier now that the digital world makes it so easy). Sri, I am sure you and I will have many battles ahead, but if I as the brand builder do my job and you, the storyteller of the world do your job, we have a unique and successful contribution to make to the fashion world. The Comité Colbert and its wise leaders were right.

Dilip Kapur is the founder of Hidesign.

JUST A LITTLE PR FOR PR

Growing up in Paris, it was impossible not to fall in love with fashion. The city has been at the heart of the industry for centuries—it is home to some of the biggest global fashion conglomerates and the birthplace of haute couture; the international influence of Parisian style is unparalleled. As a young woman, I could not escape the allure and magic of this world, and I never wanted to. In the 1980s, what made this world even more interesting was the change brought in by Japanese designers. People like Yohji Yamamoto, Rei Kawabuko, and Kenzo Takada were challenging the fundamentals of the world's fashion capital with their minimalist, utterly avant-garde designs and very curated retail experiences, which created a bridge between art and fashion.

I was sixteen when I first saw this luxurious world up close. As a Bengali girl raised in France by a musicologist father and academic mother, my ideas of fashion had been shaped by the sarees my mother wore, the salwar kameezes she dressed my sister and me in, and the streets of the cities that were the coordinates of my world—Paris, where I was born and lived in, and Kolkata, where my family's roots lie.

The glamour of Paris was, however background noise for me until one day France Grand, my formidably talented godmother, took me with her to a show by a Yohji Yamamoto—one of the most celebrated Japanese fashion designers. Decades later, I can still remember how I felt sitting at the show, watching Yamamoto's magical creations go past me. I was captivated by the draping, the silhouettes, and his use of black as a canvas. I had never known that the body could be made to look so different and so uniquely beautiful with the use of fabric and colour. What also fascinated me was how the event had been put together impeccably by a team that worked silently behind the scenes. It felt luxurious, but also deeply moving. And on that day, I added another lens to my cultural view—alongside my love for art, music, and books, a fascination for fashion and luxury took root in me.

In retrospect, I was amazed at the coming together of many cultures as assistants from Japan and teams from Paris and other countries seamlessly brought together a collection, guided by an implicit code—the one of Yohji Yamamoto's design vision. It also planted the seed of a question I still carry with me: if powerful Japanese designers could create such a momentous wave, why couldn't there be an India moment on the global fashion scene? Decades later, as I work in India, it feels like coming full circle to watch the country make the journey from being just a manufacturing hub, to becoming the birthplace of some truly inventive and incredible brands.

While writing this book, I have been both amazed and moved at the realization that the business I manage now can be traced back to an experience that was made possible by my godmother. It proves what I believe is the defining characteristic of my industry—public relations truly runs on the power and importance of relationships. From memorizing phone numbers at my first job at an agency in Paris to networking via social media today, PR has taught me how to build strong connections and leverage those in the most respectful, strategic manner.

In the twenty-five years of my career, I have worked with an agency in Paris, handled communications in-house for a large company in the US, and started my own firm—Peepul PR—in New York along with two partners in the spring of 2006. In 2007, I moved to Mumbai and moved Peepul with me. Since then, we've become a pan-Indian agency, with a presence in Delhi and Bangalore as well. Over the years, our client lists have included marquee home-grown brands, such as Good Earth, Kama Ayurveda, and Tarun Tahiliani, and international firms such as Swarovski, H&M, and Chandon for Möet Hennessy. It's the dream job I never imagined I could actually have.

Working across countries and with a really wide range of clients, I have come to the conclusion that as indispensable as my industry is, it is also really misunderstood. More often than not, people do not know what differentiates public relations from advertising or even event management. To be fair, the lines are blurred to an outsider, but PR has a very clear mandate—it is the business of storytelling, persuading people to believe in your idea or product or service, and then coordinating the flow of information through trusted, reliable mediums, whether it's a daily newspaper or an influencer.

More than ever before, I know that despite the shape-shifting nature of our digital world and the fact that every industry is constantly and rapidly evolving, the essential principles and practices of public relations are still very relevant. But often overlooked. Publicists work behind the scenes, building brands, helping individuals become brands, and holding clients' hands as they grow their businesses. It's a demanding, seemingly never-ending job, and the biggest drawback is that people don't really know how much we actually do.

Which is why I decided to write this book and do a little PR for PR. (This is my sense of humour, so I suggest you buckle up for the ride!) In all seriousness, though, whether you are a young entrepreneur without a budget to hire a publicist, you work at a successful brand and need to understand how to get the most out of your communication strategy, or you are in the business of publicity and media and just want to get a new perspective, I am speaking to you.

Because today, individuals are brands and brands are their own best ambassadors. Each one of us needs to know how to talk about ourselves and our work. We have to understand how important it is to be authentic and gritty. How to stay ahead of the game and create a legacy. And, most importantly, how to build a network that becomes our biggest strength and support.

Brand-building is no longer the domain of a few—it is the reality for us all. And if people are not talking about your brand, it may as well not exist. A decade ago, we relied on mainstream media and celebrities to create buzz. Today, we turn to traditional media, social media, influencers, micro-influencers, celebrities across all strata, and our own offline and online communities for information and endorsement. For everyone that's in this game—whatever side they're on—the playing field has become complicated and competitive. The brands that win are the most persuasive ones.

And that, really, is the trick that lies at the heart of the business of public relations. A savvy publicist helps tell just the right story to just the right people, time and time again. Which is what I hope this book will help you do. I have tapped into my own experience as a publicist and entrepreneur who works with some of India's most iconic fashion and lifestyle brands. Plus, I've spoken to friends and associates who are the brightest and the best in this industry to collate everything you need to create a pitch-perfect communications strategy that translates into every aspect of your business.

HOW TO USE THIS BOOK

My aim with *Pitch Perfect* is to offer answers and advice, share stories (the good, bad, and sometimes ugly ones), and be a friend as you build—or reinvent—your brand. By you, I mean both the new entrepreneur with stars in their eyes and fear in their hearts and the seasoned business owner flummoxed by today's crowded marketplace. I am confident that each of you will find wisdom, comfort, and humour in these pages.

In the span of my career, I have worked in several fields, but my expertise really lies in fashion, beauty, lifestyle, and luxury. Specifically, I specialize in telling the global–local story in the Indian context. What does that actually mean? That I help Indian brands create a narrative that works here and elsewhere. And I guide international brands on their Indian journeys. That is my sweet spot.

That said, everything I share can be customized by you to become relevant to whatever it is that you do. Because the principles of brand-building, storytelling, public relations, and communication are pretty universal and can be tweaked to suit any brand and situation. The bottom-line is this: if you work in fashion, beauty, or a category in the lifestyle space, this book will feel like it was written specifically for you. If not, you'll have to do some work, but you will find much material for your domain and I will not let you down.

The book is divided into five parts. The first four are named for a characteristic you need in order to build a brand people cannot stop talking about. The fifth is a playbook of wisdom and advice from industry experts. In between each part, I've added a bit of my personal journey to help you understand how I've applied all of these principles to my own work and life. We really are in this together.

Finally, please dip in and out of the chapters often and always. While it will be beneficial to read the book chronologically the first time, I hope you will keep returning to it as and when you need to. My favourite books are the ones I feel I cannot do without, and that is what I want *Pitch Perfect* to become for you.

AN ACCIDENTAL CAREER

In the 1980s, when I was slowly finding my way into the world, the It-career was information technology. Not very glamourous, but international in nature and very lucrative. It never appealed to me though. I dreamed of working in fashion, ever since I saw that Yohji Yamamoto show my godmother France Grand took me to.

I remained so captivated that France, who was working on projects with the designer, helped me get an internship at the company, and I spent a few weeks working with their in-house communications team. I would spend hours watching the business of fashion unfolding around me, and I remember being completely and utterly intimidated. I was too young and, perhaps, a bit too naive to hold my own in the very sharp and competitive world of fashion at that point in my life, but PR seemed like an excellent second choice of career.

It was a unique profession to pick—one that demands a very diverse skill-set but not much by way of degrees or specific qualifications. The best publicists have confidence, people skills, a sense of storytelling, and the ability to elevate a brand's vision.

I did not have all of these at that young age, but I, of course, have acquired them to varying degrees along the way. At Yamamoto, my internship had mostly consisted of stamping envelopes and watching other people go about their jobs. But I was a third culture kid, used to being a bit of an outsider in every situation and accustomed to finding a way to fit in wherever I went. And so, armed with the bravado of youth, I decided to make my way into public relations, landing a job with an agency that worked with tech companies in Europe in the 1990s. (See—everyone in the nineties had some connection to the IT world.)

Like every young person's first job, mine was not particularly exciting. I was asked to paste clippings of press coverage—I am really dating myself here, I know—and I hated how dull that was. Finally, one day, my to-be boss asked me to translate some text from French to English, and I found a way out of the cut-and-paste corner by doing a sloppy job of it. While it was not a particularly efficient way to get ahead, I gained an important lesson that I apply even today.

I learnt to convey my ambition by showing my skills. If I know I can land a better job, or a bigger client, or achieve a greater goal, I get to it.

Soon, I was assigned to work with one of the head publicists at the agency, a glamourous and extremely accomplished woman named Laurence Gabriel. Laurence is now the founding director of her own company called GEN-G and continues to advise companies on staying one step ahead of their game. She was terribly busy managing some of our biggest clients and had no time to train a novice, so I had to learn my job very, very quickly. This meant I worked long hours, made a ton of mistakes, picked myself up after every fall, and acquired the skill of thinking on my feet.

And that is exactly what your twenties are for, right? Getting good at your job. Swallowing your pride. Creating messes and cleaning up after yourself. Approaching everything with a beginner's mind.

Laurence, who is still a dear friend and mentor, eventually began trusting me with clients. For my part, I started learning the ropes of networking. Of talking to clients with authority and explaining what I could achieve for them and what I could not. She taught me the basics of the business, which also form the foundation of brand storytelling—finding a unique peg, crafting a narrative, and making that story interesting to a variety of people across the board, including the media and customers. The first time a journalist became a contact and wrote about a client of mine in a very well-regarded column, I felt the rush that I continue to chase—that thrill of seeing an idea take tangible shape in words and then become a conversation.

Laurence also taught me my most invaluable lesson. To listen somewhat 'laterally' during meetings. Her advice was to not interrupt, listen through what a client was sharing about his or her larger goals, and then reflect on what was at stake. Essentially, to read between the lines and always look at the bigger picture. Laurence would always revisit and translate someone's perspective into a larger vision, a stronger narrative, and even a new business strategy. She taught me to be involved in the heart of the business and not stay at the periphery, waiting for a brief. When someone shared their goals, I realized I had to think one step ahead and be ambitious for the client, just like any stakeholder would. And keep looking for the perfect story to tell.

Because, for a brand to become a part of the zeitgeist, for people to want to know more, you need to give them an authentic, but sticky, story.

It's a lesson I learnt personally, as I navigated it professionally. There was no reason why anyone would have taken a chance on a young Bengali woman in Paris, no matter how fluent my French and how rooted I felt as a born and bred Parisian. I had to take what was unique about myself and reinvent those parts of my identity that could have been seen as disadvantageous into interesting facets that people were drawn to. Here's a big confession—I am actually a shy person. I'd much rather spend an evening with my family or a close friend than in a room of strangers. And yet, I've spent more mornings, afternoons, and evenings with roomfuls of strangers for nearly three decades now. The trick lies in being curious and open so you can find the right stories to tell, conversations to craft, and information to share.

Which brings us to the first part of *Pitch Perfect*—how to use the basics of storytelling to build your DNA and find your voice.

1

Building your DNA and *finding* your voice

CHAPTER ONE

You Want to Build a Brand but Where Do You Start?

You can have a successful business without a brand, but building a brand is key to creating an experience. If you think about your business as the foundation and bare bones of a home, branding is choosing the wallpaper, picking out the furniture, and making sure you have enough flowers and art. (This is possibly why decorating homes is my second favourite thing to do.)

When you build a brand, you give your business a voice, a personality, a soundtrack, and a storytelling universe. In that sense, you brand for who you want to become and not what you are right now, as a company or an individual. People will buy into your business via your branding, and that is a key differentiator between the brands that people cannot live without and the ones they cannot remember.

I know that branding and launching a brand can sometimes sound and feel really intimidating. And so, I chatted with Lulu Raghavan, managing director, Landor & Fitch India, to tap into her decades of experience in the field and ask her how she would define a brand. 'Simply put, a brand is about associations. It is about strategically choosing what you stand for. What associations do you want to imbue in your brand name? What do you want your brand to stand for in the minds of your customers and other audiences,' she said. 'Branding is the signal system. It is the way you communicate what you stand for to the world. Your name, visual identity, verbal identity, and all the myriad touchpoints from your website to your actual product or service are opportunities to signal to the world what you stand for.'

Very early into launching Peepul in India, I met with Dilip Kapur, the founder of Hidesign, which is an iconic and much-loved leather goods and accessories brand. When I met Dilip, Hidesign was already a household brand in India. A common friend introduced us, because Dilip was looking for someone to help give the brand a fashion and lifestyle tone. When I pitched for the job, Dilip said that he was taking a very big gamble by hiring Peepul, which was a small agency at the time. But I reassured him that it was more of a calculated risk. As it turned out, banter remained a part of our working relationship, which lasted a decade and was very significant for both me and the agency.

Once we signed the papers, I was flown out to Pondicherry, where Hidesign is headquartered and Dilip lives. After our first meeting and a visit to the factory, we ate lunch with all the team members. I have never forgotten that day even though I usually forget what I ate for lunch yesterday. Dilip opened my eyes with brutal honesty to the truths of the Indian retail market, and I was brutally honest with him about Hidesign's positioning and strategy.

Working closely with him was a lesson for me in what maverick leadership means in India because Dilip marches to the beat of his own drum. But even in our first conversation, I quickly realized that his origin story of founding Hidesign in Pondicherry and working to set up international standards of production and quality with a nod to Indian aesthetics was completely lacking in the storytelling around the brand. While it was a successful brand with a large customer base, they were missing a key part of their narrative—it was a homegrown fashion label that could appeal to a much wider audience if they flipped their storytelling.

A key point here is that when Hidesign was launched—years before we started working with them—their origin story reflected international expertise, which was relevant to the zeitgeist. I chatted with Dilip to describe the brand's journey. Around the time Peepul started working with Hidesign, the popular mood celebrated local, homegrown brands and the Indian entrepreneurial spirit. We had to start telling the other side of their story. And that's exactly what we did. 'Until 1999, Hidesign was pretty much a brand abroad in several of the large western countries, but not within India or the developing countries, just around the time we started in India, we also started in some of the other countries like South Africa, the Middle East, which were also not very highly developed,' he said. 'By 2007, we'd established a long list of stores across the country in India, and India became our largest market. So Hidesign went from being a brand meant for alternative stores originally to being a brand that was accepted by international large format stores, then finally became a brand that was directly in contact with its own customers in India, which helped us eventually to also create stores internationally.'

We began helping them edit their collections in order to present to editors and stylists who would amplify our messaging. In a first for Peepul, we were also involved in product placement. I'm very proud to report that we worked with Hidesign for nearly a decade and, together, we were able to tweak its positioning as a fashion-forward lifestyle brand.

Whether you are launching a lifestyle brand or a service, my key tip is to create a story that is 360-degrees in nature, so you can spin it from any angle necessary. It also needs to be rooted in a solid idea, and concept. The important thing to remember is that what works for sales might not work for the media, and vice versa. What matters is the optics of your label—a bag that will be picked by a fashion director will reflect a collection's aesthetic or a trend. While it may not be the bestseller commercially, it will showcase an aspirational aspect of the brand. This is why it's very essential to be clear about who you are addressing and what they might find relevant and helpful.

In that vein, I have put together this list of key qualities that I find are common to the best brands:

1. The origin story is very compelling, and the entrepreneur(s) is able to tell it in a thought-provoking way that makes you want to know more.
2. They have clearly articulated their values in their product offering.
3. The customer base is very clearly identified, often backed by surgical research.
4. They fill a gap in the market, or have found their white space.
5. Alternatively, they are disruptive in the best possible way.
6. There is a visual cue—or the possibility of creating one—for their product or service.
7. While they're aware of their competition, they are not copying anyone else.
8. They make the brand aspirational in a manner that is not restricted to sales.

A FRESH NOTE

When Bombay Perfumery founder Manan Gandhi came to talk to us at Peepul in 2015, he had an idea and a concept in mind. His family had been working in the fragrance industry, and as a young entrepreneur, he wanted to launch a homegrown brand of perfumes. Now, the fragrance market is a tricky one to get into. It's very old, there are many storied brands that you have to go up against, and people tend to stay loyal to their favourite perfumes. But Manan had a compelling idea for Bombay Perfumery—the brand was Indian in its ethos but met international standards in terms of quality. (The independent homegrown fragrance market in India was quasi-non-existent then.)

To us, as publicists, Manan and Bombay Perfumery presented a very unique opportunity to create stories and build a brand narrative. India has a rich history of fragrance, but nothing contemporary to show for it. That's the gap he was aiming to fill, and we were excited to help him do that.

This is how Manan narrates his origin story: 'Indians have very strong olfactive sensibilities, and though we associate perfumes as a luxury item, fragrance permeates all facets of our day. I wanted to create a fine fragrance brand that is able to take these olfactive traditions, our beautiful ingredients and set them in a contemporary context. Developing fragrances that are championed around unique Indian ingredients, or taking moments from our daily life and deconstructing them and using them as inspiration to make distinctive fragrances.

'Similarly, with our brand world, we wanted to showcase a contemporary Indian design aesthetic, one that can be clean, minimal and modern with a subtle nod to Indian design culture, but one that doesn't use traditional Indian motifs gratuitously.

'So our goal really was quite simple: to present a modern India to the world. And we set about building our brand with this guiding principle.'

Working with Manan, my team and I created the launch strategy for Bombay Perfumery—we invited eight creative people from different fields, such as food, photography, or art, to pick one fragrance and reinterpret it in whichever way they chose. The eight fragrances—each of which combine quintessentially Indian notes such as chai, rose, pepper, ginger, and jasmine in unusual and spirited ways—were showcased at the launch event, alongside the interpretations of the chefs, photographers, etc. The evening was fun and created meaningful stories. It gave a powerful sensorial cue for a distinct India fragrance culture while celebrating the fabric of Mumbai.

I asked Manan for his point of view on working with us and on the launch.

'Creating perfumes in the lab is mostly science and some art. However, selling fragrances is all art and almost no science. To an average person, there are no quantifiable cues that make a perfume luxurious. There are no carats or thread counts or any other metrics that can be listed on a perfume bottle to showcase the fineness or craft of the product. A perfumer can make a fantastic fragrance with modest ingredients, while a marketer can also fill a fine crystal bottle with a terrible fragrance.

'A consumer buying your fragrance is buying more than the bottle and the juice inside, but what the brand represents. Fragrances are aspirational purchases as they convey your sensibilities to the world and a personal purchase as they become a part of your daily armour.

'There are almost 2,000 fine fragrances launched each year, and most of them don't work. Walking through a fragrance shop, the first thing that makes a customer stop in front of your bottle is brand recall and an almost unquantifiable resonance with your brand story.

'When I was working on building Bombay Perfumery, that was the first step we were trying to solve. How do we compete with brands that have been around for a century and how do we build credibility to stand out amongst legacy luxury brands? How do we convince a customer to stop wearing a fragrance they've worn for years and spend Rs 4000 to buy a fragrance from a completely new brand?

'So, we knew that working with a PR firm was imperative to convey our story to the world, and we sought out a partner who understood the nuances of the luxury industry while also being able understand the viewpoint of a young upcoming brand and help us hone a cohesive brand voice that conveys modernity but also seriousness of craft.

'Peepul and Srimoyi are hence a huge and irrefutable part of our success. We always think of Peepul as Employee #3 at Bombay Perfumery. They were true custodians of our brand and helped us build credibility and trust—that is so important for a category like perfumes.'

Whether you own an established business like Hidesign or are an entrepreneur with a bright idea like Manan, ask yourself:

1. What are the beliefs I am rooting this brand in?
2. What is the story I am telling?
3. What is the visual cue I want my customers to identify with me?
4. Is there anyone else who is doing something similar? If so, what can I learn from them? And what are they not doing that might work to my advantage?
5. If I have no competition to learn from in this market, can I research other markets?
6. How do I share my brand culture beyond a product?

THE POWER OF THE PERSONAL

One of the most interesting and significant developments in the world of branding is the fact that with the rise of social media, individuals are now brands in their own capacity. You might be a professional who has built a brand around your area of expertise, or an influencer, whose brand is based on your personality and unique experiences or point of view. The principles remain the same, in my opinion:

1. Treat yourself like a brand with the same non-negotiables: clarity on audience, visual identity, voice and messaging, storytelling.

2. Be clear about your values, which will help you get an authentic voice, and be consistent when you take a stand.

3. Share your passions, let people in. Imagine they are dinner guests in your home.

4. Be a good friend, be in touch regularly with a frequency that suits your profession.

5. Draw clear boundaries around your image—filter associations and collaborations through a clear lens in order to avoid controversy or misrepresentation. Conflict will get you eyeballs but eventually damage your standing.

To talk about this a bit more, I turned to two people who have built very unique, distinct personal brands.

Know thyself – Miss Malini

The first is Malini Agarwal, who started off as a radio jockey, became a columnist, and then launched a blog that became a trailblazer. She is the founder and creative director of MissMalini Entertainment and Girl Tribe by MissMalini. I asked Malini to share her top tips for those who want to build and scale a personal brand.

'Being an individual who is also a brand is such an interesting concept, one that I have learned a lot about over the last decade and a half. When I started out my career as a professional dancer and freelance copywriter, I had no idea that one day I would be known for building a personality-driven brand myself! Perhaps also because we have always thought of "brands" as products, not people.

Looking back now I realise the process of building my personal brand had kicked in years before I started officially blogging as "MissMalini". Even as a radio jockey, I had unwittingly personified myself as that "happy girl on the radio" that has the Bollywood buzz and loves to connect people. Today I look around and see the whole world of creators and influencers working hard towards crafting their own unique voice and identity, while launching their own brands, and it dawns on me how we didn't even know we were doing it, when we were doing it!

The reason I say "we" is because it truly takes an army. If you want to scale from individual to legacy you have to have the right partners, tools, industry insights and a cracker of a team, and I thankfully, have been blessed with them all. The core of the company for the last decade have been my co-founders Mike Melli (CRO), Nowshad Rizwanullah (CEO) and me, as the creative director. Plus, a legion of ninjas that make up Team MissMalini, full of hunger and hustle. Team loyalty and company culture are absolutely essential to the success of your brand. Because your team must represent your persona in everything they do. Having a team that has been with me for so long (some nearly a decade!) has been instrumental in establishing MissMalini as a bonafide brand.

But when I started it was just me, on my sofa with a laptop and no agenda or goal to turn myself into a brand. And back in 2008, I honestly would not have known where to begin to "brand" myself. But in hindsight not having that agenda is one of the best things I did and can honestly attribute a large part of our success to that too.

So, let me take you through five things that I believe make a solid brand and the highs and lows of having experienced them all.

Authenticity

I cannot stress this enough. Being authentic is at the core of any brand. Consider it the beating heart of your brand. When you stop being authentic, you die. (Or rather less dramatically, your brand does.)

Highs – It is somewhat easier to be authentic because, well, you just need to be you. You are already a whole person, now just spill the reali-tea! People have a range of emotions, and brand loyalists are those who connect and relate specifically to yours, making you an integral part of their own life.

With MissMalini, I always wrote the way I spoke, created a virtual avatar, poured my entire personality into her and boom! I was suddenly living an entire virtual life in the body of an animated illustration who was still very much me. Whenever I had to make a brand decision or craft my communication, the first question I would ask myself is, "What would MissMalini do or say?"

Lows – This is really not something I personally think of as a low, but I can appreciate how being a brand can get tiresome. When you sign up to be the brand yourself, your life is not really entirely yours anymore. Your life is now content, constantly on display. You will get your fair share of criticism along with the praise and everything you do will impact the perception of your brand. That can be both exhilarating and exhausting.

Uniqueness

I truly believe that any successful brand, whether product or person needs to find its USP and carve its own niche. Most successful brands start out by asking, "What is the gap in the market? How am I addressing it and how am I doing it differently, or better than anyone else?" The same applies to personal branding.

Highs – It was extremely exciting to come into a market that was absolutely untapped for the role of content creator/influencer. In fact, neither of those terms existed back then. I was just a friendly voice in entertainment personified through the eyes of a millennial Indian girl who loves everything Bollywood, fashion and pop culture—your virtual BFF of sorts. Someone to help you navigate through your fashion and beauty choices while keeping you abreast of pop culture in an unintimidating way. A brand that responded to your questions like a friend and took you along for the ride on her own Bollywood adventures as a fly on the wall. Something that traditional entertainment media was not really doing.

Lows – It took a while for people to understand what I did for a living (my parents included). A lot of people thought that all I did was go to parties and couldn't quite understand the business or the brand aspect. Again, it came down to persistence and the time it takes for a market to mature enough to accept an entirely new industry. Today being a content creator or influencer is immediately recognized as a very viable and fulfilling career. It took a while for advertisers to understand the brand value of an individual and to consider diverting marketing budgets towards them. I must give full credit here to my co-founder and CRO Mike Melli. He made it his personal mission to educate brands on the value of influencer marketing and is significantly responsible for the myriad opportunities in the industry today.

Integrity

Being your own brand comes with a lot of power and, as Spiderman said, "With great power, comes great responsibility!" You have the power to influence millions of people with the choices you make, and we have seen in no uncertain terms how this can go south really fast if you abuse that power. It is extremely important that your brand stands for something all the time, not just when it's convenient or Instagram-worthy.

Highs – For me it became clear early on that I wanted to celebrate the entertainment industry that we have all grown up loving, without negativity. This is why we avoided focusing on "fashion policing" or digging up personal dirt. There are enough places to gossip about unvalidated rumours. Again, I say we because, by this point, the MissMalini brand was no longer just one person. In fact, a slew of writers were contributing to that voice and so I established a rule that we would only ever write what we could say to someone's face. My greatest learning has been that when you expand your personal brand, it is imperative that your entire team knows and upholds your personal values, because eventually, everything that is said or done under your brand will be attributed to you. Having witnessed the lengths to which people will go to convince you to promote their products and holding firm on our values even in the face of dollar signs is something we are very proud of. Case in point, never caving to the "fairness cream" mafia. No matter how much business we declined.

Lows – When the #MeToo movement finally made its way over to India I realised that we were part of an industry that is notorious for its crimes against women. And yet, we had unwittingly turned a blind eye or not called out enough people that were clearly part of the problem. At that point we probably convinced ourselves that it was all so much bigger than and we would be eclipsed in war. But I can say, hand on heart, that we have made every effort and endeavour since that realisation to support and uplift women and stand up for what is right and fight the good fight.

The last two personal branding tips are really what I call "hygiene" when it comes to building a brand, at least a personal brand on social media.

Innovation and Agility

We have seen platforms come and go and technology make leaps and bounds. It is absolutely key to keep in touch with trends and not to put all your eggs in one basket. Or on one social media platform! Build a brand that surpasses the medium it is on and you're golden. When people no longer attach your name to the platform that you started on, you know you've built a legacy brand.

Engagement

Personal brands are built on relationships, both B2B (business to business) and P2P (person to person.) Now more than ever people are craving to be heard, to be seen, to be validated. And now more than ever we have all the tools to do so at a scale that was not previously or humanly possible. So, engage! Put the "social" back in social media. Talk back to the people who look up to you, admire you, follow you. Unsee the numbers and see the people and always ask yourself how you would interact with them in real life. Would you drop an emoji and run? Or would stop and have a conversation.

For us, our solution was the creation of Girl Tribe by MissMalini, our own social media app that puts people and positivity first. Girl Tribe is a place that helps women connect online as they would in real life, putting empathy and kindness first. This has been invaluable in building my personal brand, allowing me to engage directly with my followers in an authentic, unique, trusted and innovative way – which, if you've been paying attention, is everything you really need to succeed.'

Take a Chance on You

My friend Ashiesh Shah is an architect celebrated for his design projects across the country. He has built a very specific and focused personal brand that serves his work very well. We had a conversation about how and why he did that.

When you have to brand yourself, as an individual professional with an area of expertise, how do you approach that?

Focusing on your strengths and what sets you apart in your profession is the first step to developing efficient brand communication. Next, find your ideal audience. With design, which is my industry, I have found that because it is a rather subjective and individualistic profession, positioning yourself within the market is the most important thing. The spaces your design set a signature style, which, more often than not, become your distinct form of brand communication

What role does social media play, versus that of traditional media? Would you say one matters more than the other?

Social media and traditional media both cater to different audiences and work fabulously based on the target audience.

In my perspective, traditional media tends to have a stronger backing and is perceived in higher regard. Social media has a wider reach. I think a balance of both is key and the choosing one over the other depends on your target audience.

Do you invest in creating your own content, and is that worth the while?

It is definitely worth investing in because creating your own content is the basis for good storytelling. In design, the content we showcase ends up being a valuable resource for the studio as a whole and very important in our process of development, owing to the larger story of the atelier.

CHAPTER TWO

Know Your Audience

If you don't have a customer, you don't have a brand. It's as simple as that. Whether you're a start-up relying on the love and support of friends and family, or you're an established company with a firmly loyal audience behind you, a brand is a brand only when people are aware of it and spend their time and/or money on it.

In today's world, I would argue that building, nurturing, and growing your customer base is as crucial as perfecting your product or service. And it requires just as much time, effort, and patience. Because engagement is no longer a linear word or process—the way brands function has undergone a fundamental shift, especially since COVID-19 altered our lifestyles drastically in 2020. And, of course, the result of this is that the way people engage with brands is also being transformed. We always ask ourselves, is the conversation led by necessity or desire?

One of the most interesting observations I have made over the years has been how brands have had to change the way they speak to a customer. And this is a good thing, believe me. When I started working in PR, it was all fairly straightforward and standard—you wrote press releases, you built relationships with the right journalists who could help spread the word about your client and their brand, and you waited for the press to mention the product or service in order to make the customer aware of it. Now, it's a completely diverse and exciting universe in which an audience does not just mean the customer who buys the product or service but also the ones who might follow you on social media and support you in other ways.

At Peepul, for example, we find two categories of clients coming to us—those that are just starting out and those that have a target audience but want to grow it or add another layer to it.

SHINY, HAPPY, NEW

Whatever the product or service is that you are introducing, my advice is to start by talking to a community of potential customers and supporters. This can be as small as a group of twenty-five people that you know and trust, or you can enlist the help of an agency that can poll larger numbers. Either way, what you want to know is this: do people feel the lack of this product or service? If so, it means that there is a desire for it, and what you need to do is seduce them to buy it from you. Alternatively, do you need to create that desire for them?

One of the most exciting launches we've worked on at Peepul was that of Chandon, which is a range of sparkling wines introduced to India by Moët Hennessy in 2013. Our job, when we were brought on board, was to build an appetite for sparkling wine and then raise the brand recognition for Chandon. Since we were working with a global brand that could give us access to facts and figures that underlined the appeal and desirability of the product, that's where we started our journey. Sharing this information with key members of the press, prestigious publications, and the right tastemakers was a good way to spread the word to begin with. I just want to add here that we were on board nearly ten months before launch. And this is something I say to every CLIENT who wants us to work on a launch. The earlier we are included in the process, the better it is. The lead-up is as important as a launch.

From a strategic point of view, we took a step back from the product. We had to educate people about a new category, almost like Bombay Perfumery did, in a sense. We had to build a foundation for the culture of sparkling wine, which was quite a novel product at the time.

There was a clear desire for it and enough of an appetite that we could tap into. The route we decided to take at Peepul for our clients was to create a lifestyle experience around sparkling wine—from events to the kinds of stories we pitched to the press, this was our goal. For example, we worked with leading mixologists who demonstrated how to make cocktails using Chandon wines. At events, we identified celebrities who embodied a glamorous but fun lifestyle that we knew our target audience aspired to. Piece by piece and over time, we put together a picture of the Chandon universe.

The reason I am emphasizing the fact that it takes time is because it does. There's no other way to say this—spend time on your launch (or relaunch) and get every bit of the puzzle in place. When a client comes to us with a brand-new company or vertical, we actually prefer having three to six months pre-launch to make sure everything is as it should be. I like to call this the seed period because that's what you're doing—conversing with potential customers, scoping out the market to make sure you have all your ducks in order, getting the branding and visual identity together, and creating a cohesive big-picture plan.

At this point, I want to talk about two non-negotiables I look for when working with a new product or service:

Brand purpose and values. Of all the pieces of this puzzle, this one is both the simplest and the most complex. So, I turned to Lulu for help again with a simple question: what should people think about first when they want to launch a new product or service?

She said, 'They should think about why the business needs to exist in the first place. Why does the world need another fashion brand, another e-commerce start-up, another bakery?'

'What is the unique value they provide to their customers? How are they meaningfully relevant? And how are they going to be different to their competitors. Working out the very purpose of the brand—an existential question to answer—and the value proposition are the first things to be done.'

'The value you provide is what will attract customers in the first place and also keep them in your fold. When thinking about value, think hard about the benefits (emotional and functional) you provide over and above the product/service's features and other attributes.'

Working in PR, I know that this is a key part of translating a brand's purpose and making it tangible. Its purpose and values drive storytelling, experiences, and audience building. At Peepul, once we know what a brand stands for and what it delivers on, it becomes easier for us to layer in emotion and texture to create a real universe around it. For example, Good Earth, which is one of our clients, has over the years built a brand around the origin of a craft, their own discovery of it, the creation of a collection, the design process, and their interpretation of it. The fact that all of this comes through in every aspect of their brand story and storytelling adds layers of romance to a Good Earth product. And by the time you walk into a store or visit their website, you are primed for it.

When I asked Anita Lal, founder of Good Earth, how the brand has achieved this, she stressed on the brand's purpose and values, rooted in her own vision, which serve as guideposts. 'Ever since I started Good Earth, I understood instinctively the importance of creating products for a lifestyle that is relevant in the Indian context', she said. 'Something that works with our seasons, our love for colour and the way we live', she said. 'I felt we should create designs and products through our own Indian prism and not follow any particular Western trend; [these are] products that are of the highest quality with a timeless universal appeal. The experience of owning and using them must be elevated. My vision is that our designs always be thoughtful and our products mindfully made, preferably by hand and in collaboration with India's vast, diverse, and amazing skilled community of artisans. This is our heritage, and we must celebrate it in the best way we can.'

A visual identity. The number one question I ask clients—and my team will vouch for this—is, 'What do you want people to visualize when they think of your brand?' For example, you say Tiffany and I think blue. Or when you mention Good Earth, I immediately have an image of Mughal motifs. Brands become iconic for their logos, packaging, colours, certain products, or their design aesthetic.

I highly recommend working with a professional branding agency or individual for this, and you can choose either according to your budget. Big bucks do not always equal excellent results.

Remember that your visual identity has to tie in with your purpose and values, and it has to appeal to your ideal customer. They're all interconnected. Again, go back to your sample group and ask them what appeals to them from a line-up of prototypes. How does it make them feel when they see your logo or packaging or branding colours?

A clear point of view. Don't be afraid to take a stand and do something unique. While data polling and getting a bunch of opinions are all very useful and necessary, you don't have to follow the herd. As long as you see white space in the market for yourself and you are convinced that there are people who want what you're selling, even if they don't know it yet, do what you need to do. I am a big fan of new ideas and bold approaches, so I'll always encourage you not to play safe to fit in or toe the line.

A SECOND LIFE

I'm always interested in watching how established brands reinvent themselves for new markets via new products or services or by tapping into a new customer base. When Jean-Claude Biguine entered India with a chain of salons in major cities in 2006, I was very intrigued to see how they presented themselves to a country that was bursting with aspiration and had a huge appetite. Back in France, JCB (if I may call it that) is a very competent chain of salons that gets the job done with no fuss or frill. In India, however, their positioning was elevated from day one. They spoke to the customer who wanted the experience of going to the salon to be more luxurious but not inaccessible. They speak to a completely different audience in India from the one that engages with them in France. It was such a clever move to make, and it's a great example of how to switch your image around to give the brand a new lease of life.

A brand that I think has also done this very well, but within the same markets, is Amrapali, with Tribe. While the legacy (and umbrella) brand has built its stellar reputation for its specific aesthetic, design language, and quality, Tribe is its younger, and more experimental avatar. I spoke with Tarang Arora, whose family owns Amrapali and who has played a pivotal role in launching and running Tribe, about why they made the decision to diversify. He said, 'The whole idea of creating a new brand under the flagship of Amrapali was to welcome an entirely new segment of customers. People who like to express themselves through jewellery are our main clients. While Amrapali has its own aura and essence, Tribe is for a free soul. Each and every piece we create at Tribe is so expressive and beautiful, but we offer these at nominal prices. With this brand, we are able to focus on a different segment of the audience, which prefers experimental designs that are contemporary and unique, but not expensive.'

Having worked with Tarang and his team on Tribe, I know that while they stay true to the core values of Amrapali, they are not afraid to think outside the box and have fun, which brings a different energy to the brand. Especially when it comes to reinventing or relaunching a brand or introducing a new label or vertical, what a publicist does is bridge the gap between the brand and its ideal customer. As Tarang described it, working with a PR agency helped them tell their story better. 'A team which is eloquent can make the world perceive exactly what you want them to, which is very crucial for any business. It takes a lot of persuasion to make someone else align with your thought process. So having a team that comprehends your ideas and connects them with the world outside is very important. In order to get to know your target audience and understand how to reach them, it is very important to have a set of people who can give you the relevant strategy and execute it.'

BEING SEEN AND HEARD

I'll talk about this much more in the next chapter and others, of course, but once you know your customer and you have your basics in place, start thinking about how you're going to communicate with them. Will social media be your primary and maybe even only platform for a couple of months? Or do you want to engage with a PR agency or an individual publicist to help you start a dialogue with your target audience, mainstream media, and influencers?

The answer lies in a combination of factors. A key one is the budget you have at your disposal, and another important point to consider is at what point it would serve you best to have an external agency or individual come in to help you. There are several brands who may not be served best by having a PR agency because the founder or team are the best storytellers, and having someone else in the mix might actually end up being counterproductive.

If you are looking to hire a PR agency right at the start, make sure you ask around to find an agency or individual who works in the market you're looking to make a mark in. As a rule of thumb, a boutique brand is best paired with a smaller agency while larger players go well together. Look for someone who understands you instinctively and whose ideas match yours. Because what a good publicist will do for you is help you speak to your audience in a better, more engaging, and more consistent manner. And at the end of the day, everyone wants that ally.

CHAPTER THREE

What Do Voice and Messaging Mean?

I don't know about you, but when I was growing up, the only way I saw a brand communicate directly with its customers was through advertising—print, radio, or television. Iconic ads were burnt into our minds, and we still remember those brands for a jingle or a tag line or a model. Now, however, communicating with your customer is a 24/7, 365-day exercise, and it's non-negotiable. Whether someone follows your brand and/or team on Instagram, likes your Facebook page, subscribes to your YouTube channel, visits your website, or signs up for your newsletter, you have to find a way to stay in conversation with them at all times. Which is why voice and messaging are so key to brand-building in this day and age. It is part and parcel of your personality and identity.

BACK TO BASICS

So let's make this fun. Take a minute to think about what your favourite brand sounds like and what it says. With too many brands swimming in my head (professional hazard), I asked my husband Sourabh. He thought of Paul Smith, which he feels is clear about its stand towards colour. It is edgy but humble, and while slightly irreverent, it still is a classic brand. Paul Smith has fun with fashion, and its clients do, too.

And this is what Lulu Raghavan of Landor had to say when I chatted with her about it. 'Voice is the unique way in which you express the personality of the brand. In today's cluttered communication landscape, a clear and distinct brand voice helps you stand out and connect emotionally with your audiences. I love the IndiGo voice—it is there everywhere from their airline code (6E—how brilliant is that!) to "Nut Case" their box of nuts sold inflight! If you don't have a voice, you risk being bland and being lost in the sea of sameness.'

With your voice, you tell your potential or existing customer what you stand for and what they can expect from you. You can communicate your message and your ethos, which are both essential for you to find and build the right client base for your brand. One way to do this is to hire a professional or engage with an agency, which can then guide you, work closely with you, and sharpen the voice until it's perfect. This is one aspect of brand-building for which I actually highly recommend working with a third party because you will benefit from their expertise and impartial point of view. It can feel difficult to wade through this process on your own simply because you (and your team) might be too close to the brand to stay objective and separate the good from the bad. I have found over the years that nine out of ten times, the most clever, articulate brands have worked with professionals at some point to get their branding right.

That said, if you are starting out or rebranding and just don't have the time or resources or intention to work with a professional person or agency, here's a simple solution. Think about these questions. What if your brand was a person? What would they sound like? What would their personality be like? For example, Disney is happy. Nike sounds like a go-getter. Apple inspires confidence and efficiency.

How would you like to communicate? Who are you talking to and why are people listening to you? Think about other brands in that genre or category and what they sound like. What can you do to stand apart? How do you want to make customers feel with your voice? What does your brand have to say for itself? Try different ideas on for size and run them past a small, trusted group of people who can give you clear and honest feedback.

WHAT'S THE BIG IDEA?

When the idea for Peepul came to me, I was with my mother in the countryside outside Kolkata, in a simple homestay. I'd just been part of putting together a hugely publicized, high-profile wedding. My cortisol and adrenaline were sky-high, but I felt drained and completely uninspired. Taking me away to a calmer place had been my mother's idea, and after a few days, I felt relieved of that sense of doing too much but not doing enough at the same time. I knew I had to change how I worked, and build something for myself, but ideas evaded me. And, I am not kidding, I was lying under a peepul tree, with my head in my mother's lap, when it hit me like a bolt of lightning. I had to start a PR agency of my own and I wanted to call it Peepul. I could not have made up a better origin story had I tried, I promise you.

The more I thought about it, the more it made sense to me to meld my Bengali inner life with my transcontinental professional journey, and create an agency that worked with Indian brands which were trying to create a niche for themselves in the US market. That was Peepul's first iteration. And the name made sense—like a tree, I wanted my company to have deep and solid roots that supported lush growth. Plus, I liked the pun, which worked as a nod to the fact that publicity is people-centric in every way. Finally, when I tried the name out on friends, they found it to be a conversation starter. From there, the voice I developed was strong but unafraid of fun or whimsy—a bit irreverent but always professional—and rooted in the Indian experience while spanning cultures and countries.

Over the years, of course, Peepul's voice as an agency has evolved, but I am proud of the fact that it still stays true to the core idea that came to me that afternoon.

CHANGE IS CONSTANT

This is an important point to remember—the voice will grow and change with time, but it needs to always align with your brand's DNA. It also needs to lend itself to storytelling and messaging across mediums. Because every brand now has the luxury of speaking to targeted audiences, making sure you sound appealing to them is even more important than ever. Your brand's voice cannot just sell a product or service—it has to sustain values, conversations, long-term relationships and be versatile enough to navigate all mediums. In a noisy, crowded world, online and offline, it has to hold its own and attract an audience that is interested not only in listening to you but also buying from you.

Here, I want to talk for a quick minute about a niche brand that I think uses its voice to tell stories very well. Peter D'Ascoli runs his eponymous handcrafted textile business out of India, working and retailing with some of the most respected and select outlets across the world. On his Instagram, he not only shares snippets of his work but also a ton of interesting information about history, art, culture, architecture, etc., which are part of his universe.

'The D'ASCOLI brand is an outgrowth of an aesthetic sensibility that has been cultivated over the past thirty years and represents the personal vision of the creators of the company,' said Peter, when I spoke to him about how the brand's communication and voice have evolved. 'There is no science or guide to inform us as to what is and is not an appropriate direction for our design and marketing material, this aesthetic "filter" is established each day with the creative direction administered by the design studio when deciding on colours, designs, graphics, and the ideas driving product and marketing materials.'

He cautions entrepreneurs to make sure they are ready on all fronts to launch a brand: 'Don't do it without the requisite experience and understanding. All too often, we see young people launching companies before they have formed a strong opinion or inner knowledge of what they want to say. A brand reflects the personality of whomever is managing it, and this personality, this vision must come from within. Without clarity and depth, one cannot create a strong brand.'

WHAT DO YOU HAVE TO SAY FOR YOURSELF?

And here's where voice segues into messaging. Again, I asked Lulu to simplify this for us, and she said, 'Messaging is a manifestation of the brand's purpose through the verbal touchpoints. Every message matters because it is a unique opportunity to say something meaningful and reinforce the brand's unique associations in the minds of the consumer. Messaging is one of the most underrated and overlooked avenues for brand-building. Sweat this channel and you are sure to reap rewards in terms of building imagery for your brand.'

For me and my team, as publicists, messaging is the first and most important function. As soon as we engage with a client, we have a laundry list of questions and thoughts on the subject:

- What are the topics that give this brand a unique identity?
- How can the brand talk to audiences on social media or any other digital platform?
- What can we do to the voice to optimize messaging?
- How can the people behind the brand be spotlighted?
- How often should they be talking to followers/clients?

Before we can get to any of this, though, we need to understand the brand's mission and core message, which should emphasize the why—why does this brand matter, and why should people listen to it? For example, Bumble's messaging can be overtly feminist, but its voice stays light and easy. Good Earth, on the other hand, focuses on creating a sense of wonder with its messaging, and its voice is knowledgeable and has gravitas. Both are very distinctive and very successful in their spheres; it is because they are so clear about what they sound like and what they want to say, that we can do our jobs without any dissonance. We know which publications or digital influencers to approach and how to spin the storytelling to keep it authentic and effective.

Deepika Gehani, senior vice-president of PR, marketing & design at Reliance Brands, emphasizes this too: 'The brands that achieve their status and are loved worldwide because of what the brand represents have a clear brand voice and set guidelines to ensure that they retain it. The brands that we work with are very strict about these aspects and ensure that each and every customer interaction should embody the brand values to the core and every customer experience should be consistent with their expectation of the brand irrespective of which part of the world it comes from. Hence, they monitor everything from the shop appearance, window display, staff hires, uniforms, seasonal campaign communications, strategy, all of which is approved by their global office and then executed.'

Whether you're doing this for the first time or you're tweaking and polishing for an existing brand, this is a useful set of questions and exercises to work through:

- List your vision for the brand, both in the short and long run.
- With these in mind, how would you like your consumer to respond to your product/service/social media?
- If your product were a person, what are the five distinctive qualities that would set it apart?
- How do you define your ideal customer or target audience? Get granular—who are they, where do they live, what do they like, and which other brands do they patronize?
- How will your messaging resonate with them?
- What are the specific results you wish to achieve with this messaging?
- What is the kind of community you want to build and universe you want to create for them? Here, it helps to think visually. Even if you don't have a brick-and-mortar store and may never open one, think about what it would look like. The colours, the decor, the experience you would provide a customer who walks into it—how can you translate all of this into the messaging?

When voice and messaging come together, they create magic. They help you articulate your brand values to your customer in a way that creates a true connection. People invest in and champion brands that make them feel the way they want to feel. So, I would encourage you to spend real time and effort on these to be able to build a strong communication system, inside and out.

Doing It Your Way

Tarun Tahiliani is a legend in the Indian fashion business. And with good reason. He was one of the pioneers in retail with his multi-designer store, Ensemble, which now has a pan-India presence, and he has been instrumental in bringing the industry together cohesively. For his own eponymous brand, TT, as he is popularly called, has created a distinct voice without following a rulebook. The brand's voice and personality echo its journey and evolution. I requested Tarun to share his story in his own words.

'To be perfectly honest, we started Tarun Tahiliani, the brand with just passion for what we were doing. And that is the best way to start.

'I love design and fashion, and there were really only two or three worthy stores in a country like India that showcased fashion well. So we began Ensemble in 1987 with the desire to showcase talent and innovation in a changing landscape. From there, I discovered that my real love was design, so I slowly spent more time doing that. Finally, I decided to study technique to make real progress.

'From there, I moved to Delhi, and we started the Fashion Design Council of India, and then went on to showcasing contemporary Indian fashion all over the globe. And really, by and by, we found our own Indian voice, which I call the new voice of tradition. While I have all the respect and time for tradition and I value what this country stands for and its great heritage, I also feel that there are inflection points in a country's history, which we've been a part of because it coincided with the opening up of India, the acceptance of Western ideas of cut and construction, and a very global Indian finding their place in the new world. While it might be nice to harbour tradition, there are always room and need for modernity, and that's what we've pushed to find. It doesn't make traditional bad. It just finds a modern way of using things to fit into a new life.

'Having said that, I probably am a little more old-school, in that I live in my own world, read what I want to, and engage in silence with our culture and with museums across the world. I've grown up at a time when people understood luxury at a very deep level. And while that may not be the world right now, I think with affluence and exposure, people will find their way. So social media kind of bypassed me initially. And I have very little time, personally, for what "celebrities" pretend to say or do in borrowed clothes or the general hype that social media can create. But the beauty of social media is that it goes everywhere and percolates to everyone.

'So it took us a while to understand what the voice of Tarun Tahiliani needed to be. Since clothing, its quality, techniques and fit are, to me, as important as the designer, their relevance had to be the tone of our social media to begin with. Storytelling needed wonderful imagery and amazing attention to detail. And the part that I was most comfortable with was what we call behind-the-scenes, because there is nothing enacted for social media. We show it as it is, we show our processes, and we show the beautiful factory where our samples are made. So, in that respect, it's been wonderful.

'We no longer have to rely on somebody else's filter if and when they want to tell a story. We can tell it in snippets as an ongoing event ourselves. But like everything in life, that can be an overkill. So I think we strive to strike a balance. I do not feel the need for it to be about me personally. I do not want to project anything, and I'm certainly not going to pose with people non-stop and put these pictures up on social media.

'The COVID-19 pandemic forced this issue further because now social media is the most effective way of reaching out and talking to your customers. All the above-mentioned attributes that we believe in are more important than ever before. It's difficult to speak so many different audiences. I think that basically you have to have a voice and with your ideology, it will string together an audience of people who have the same values or who respond to yours. Within that, we might talk to young people who want to be brides and grooms, or we might talk to an older, more sophisticated customer. But it's a design philosophy that really unites everything. And I think if a brand is authentic, then it'll have a certain kind of a following.

'More than ever before, value, voice, and messaging are very, very important to a brand's journey. For people who are going to follow your storytelling all the time and take the trouble to read or listen to you, what one says and what one does with the clothes, how they're made, and what they represent are all very important parts of the final story. Consistency will make for longevity.

'Inevitably, messaging changes from time to time. I'm constantly told that people want to see more and hear more from me, but I'm happy to do it as long as it's relevant to the story that's being told at that moment. There has to be a balance. I design and make beautiful clothes, and people should wear them if they're relevant to them. And that would be the simplest, most classic way in which people should engage with the brand—what does it mean to them, and what they feels when they're in the clothes. I'm aware that there are many tricks now to layer on top of these, but honestly for me, I am a little uncomfortable doing much more than the classical way of communication with the exception of allowing people access to the behind-the-scenes to see how the brand designs and manufactures.

'Working with a publicist is very important. They can give you an objective view of what you are doing. I might think I am doing something correctly and be completely off the mark. So if you have a publicist to screen you, they push you to do new things and make you aware of the consequences of your choices. Like everything else in life, it's like having a seasoned friend whom you need to take advice from. Especially when we are doing big shows and events, the publicists help us to coordinate and think out of the box. And, that is invaluable.'

CHAPTER FOUR

Getting Your Storytelling Right

When you are at an event—whether that's a friend's dinner party or a networking evening with peers—what do you notice in people? Maybe it's an outfit that was particularly stylish or the fact that someone had lovely hair or was very elegant. And what makes you remember them the next day? It's what they had to say for themselves, yes? The conversation you had that was funny or enlightening. An anecdote they shared that stayed in your mind. We remember people for the stories they tell. And that's true for brands, too.

The maverick and very successful marketer and author Seth Godin says we now live in a 'connection economy', and what sets us apart from the Industrial Age is the fact that nothing is standardized anymore. Mass media, communication, marketing, and advertising are not the norm any longer. People now listen to those they want to listen to. They will click on the links they choose to and open the emails they feel matter to them. To communicate effectively and successfully, brands (and individuals) need to build trust, create meaningful connections, ask for permission to speak to someone, and exchange ideas in a generous and unique manner. You cannot stick to a formula. You cannot do anything that's just enough—you have to bake the extraordinary into the routine. And you need to think out of the box as the rule and not the exception.

What all of this boils down to for brands, in my opinion, is storytelling. Now that you have a voice and are clear on your messaging, what do you have to say for yourself? And I want to dispel a common mistake I see people making these days of assuming that storytelling is just for social media posts. It's really not. From the text on your website to the bio on your social media and the content you share online and offline, brand storytelling is another foundational aspect you cannot afford to take lightly.

Today's consumer no longer makes buying decisions based on price or product range. They are driven by emotions and experiences, and they want to understand a brand's values, provenance, and purpose before investing time or money in its products and services. Take for example the fact that if you want to buy a simple white t-shirt, you can choose to either go to a high-street brand, or support a sustainable organic label, or even buy that t-shirt with a high-luxe branded price tag. Each of these brands has a story to tell, and they have to share it consistently across platforms to not just reach their ideal customer, but also retain their attention and support.

When Deepika Gehani was talking to me about brand messaging, she also outlined the importance of knowing what to say, and who to say it to: 'Many brand success stories are testament to the effectiveness of storytelling. Every brand essentially has its unique strengths, an angle, or a story, and customers want to hear about it. Sometimes it is the brand heritage and the journey, or sometimes the product may be state of art and innovative and therefore inspiring. This hook is an effective strategy as it compels people to make a purchase. Storytelling also helps in building brand loyalty with customers. However, there needs to be a healthy balance, and more often than not brands forget that the narratives need to resonate with your target audience. If a brand story is disconnected from the people that you want to influence, even the greatest version of it will not suffice.'

In all her years of experience, she finds that 'honesty is what makes a brand communication successful. Any global or local or high-end luxury brand can plan the most outrageous campaigns, but if the quality of the product does not deliver, it is definitely a disaster in making. You have to focus on three things—your product and its USP, which clearly needs to be the highlight of your communication; understanding your customer; and planning, because without it, even the best ideas are unsuccessful.'

As much as it is tempting to stick to a formula or try pleasing an algorithm, your brand story needs a strong foundation and a lot of thought. So where do you start?

UP CLOSE AND PERSONAL

Think about your customer and what they expect from you. This is an important aspect to get very clear on because it helps you decide your storytelling pillars, the social media platforms you need to be on, and the offline strategy you have to employ. Chinmayee Manjunath, who helped me write this book and works with brands on content and communication strategy, has a couple of firm guidelines to help her clients understand their audience:

- How old is your ideal customer? This is absolutely the first step, because once you know the age group of the person you want to target, you can understand what kind of storytelling will appeal to them.

- How and where does your ideal customer consume content? This immediately helps you decide whether you need to be making Reels on Instagram or if your money is better spent doing in-store events, and maybe emailing a fortnightly newsletter. Or perhaps you need to do nothing online and focus on traditional media.

- What are the other brands that your customer supports, and is there a gap between what your competition offers them and what you can? Create a unique storytelling universe, and while there is always some overlap and repetition within an industry, getting very clear on your USP will help you stand out regardless.

- Is there a category of content or information that you know they would benefit from, even if they don't know it themselves? Say, for example, you own a florist business and specialize in creating bespoke arrangements. What might be nice is to look at the mythology, healing properties, characteristics, and attributes of the flowers that you use. You could also share your own process of how you source flowers, what draws you to certain blooms, and guide your clients on how to choose flowers based on more than just colour and appearance. This adds many layers to what could be a very cut-and-dried process.

Next, you need to align your messaging—which the previous chapter helps you strategize on—with your storytelling pillars. Broadly, these are the most common five pillars, but you will need to tweak them according to your business and what your brand stands for.

1. Inspirational: Happy, cheerful, bright, and uplifting messaging, which is something everyone can and should benefit from. This is when you use quotes from famous people, create stunning flat lays, shoot beautiful visuals, and feature influencer shout-outs, for instance.

2. Educational: To build thought leadership, facilitate knowledge and create an environment for people to learn about your brand and your industry is essential. Content under this pillar includes tips and tricks, video trainings, and stories of culture and heritage.

3. Conversational: Engagement is always key, whether that means comments on a post or chatting with clients on the phone or via video calls. Your aim here is to spark organic interaction via events, giveaways, contests, and polls.

4. Community-building: This pillar is especially important on social media because it helps you convey the lifestyle you envision for your clients, share behind-the-scenes of the brand, and foster personal connections with your content.

5. Commercial: Fairly straightforward and essential to your marketing are calls to action, announcements of new launches or sales, and conducting lives on social media or events offline.

TALKING BUSINESS

As publicists, storytelling is key to what we do because we're acting as a bridge between the brand and the world. What they choose to share on social media, their website, all communication collateral, and their interactions with the press are important to our work. When talking to a client about their storytelling, I also find that it helps to tailor it to the life phase of a brand or its culture. If you are a start-up, for instance, you might need to educate your customer about your brand or category (like Bombay Perfumery and Chandon did). And if your brand has been around a while but has to establish itself more firmly in the minds of your clients, I would recommend focusing on conversational and commercial content.

Two golden rules—find the middle path between serving your audience and meeting your marketing and sales needs. Telling stories can be meaningful, wonderful, and fun even on its own, but for a brand, it has to tie back into the business. Secondly, always keep your eye on the bigger picture, so plan your storytelling calendar for the year or at least two quarters at a time. Match this with your marketing and sales calendars and create a Venn diagram of how your content will serve other functions and vice versa. As Chinmayee points out, your content has to match your commerce or there is no point to it at all.

When she and I chatted about this subject, we found that while her approach is more editorial and mine is more PR-centred, the common ground is that brands have to tell stories that fit into their DNA. Being trendy does not work, and neither does being too commercial. Let me take the example here of Raw Mango, the label founded and run by Sanjay Garg, who is a textile designer and was a client of ours at Peepul. The brand is coveted for its stunning use of traditional weaves and colour. Over the years, Raw Mango's storytelling has become singular and instantly identifiable because right from the models they use to the way their campaigns are shot, there is a unique aesthetic that is now entirely their own. The stories the brand tells, from Sanjay's interviews in traditional media to the text they write on their Instagram, and the way the stores are designed all celebrate weaves, crafts, and colours, it's all very educational, emotional, and inspiring. And unique.

CHANGING THINGS UP

Often brands realize that they have to switch their storytelling around to reflect a rebrand, pivot, or even the next stage in their journey. While it can seem tricky or daunting to do this, it's not. I recommend revisiting the exercise to determine your audience first. Are you still speaking to the same person, or is your target audience now a little or a lot different? In some cases, it might just be that your customer has stayed with you, but, just like your brand, they have evolved too. In whichever scenario you find yourself, repeating the whole exercise with your new goals in mind helps.

For example, if your brand is now five years old, your pillars need to change, as do your voice and messaging, to reflect that. Or if yours is a legacy brand that has launched a new vertical, you might want to stay rooted in the overall brand values, but create fresh language and messaging specific to the new business.

'Content Is Not Just a Word'

Whenever I think of storytelling, I immediately think of Good Earth. The brand, which turned twenty-five in 2021, has perfected the art of telling stories seamlessly across platforms, both online and offline. What is particularly impressive to me is how they have successfully created a brand language and are able to offer the same experience whether you are at their stores or on their Instagram account. To understand how they approach storytelling, I requested Shagun Singh, head of marketing and communications, Good Earth, to write a little note about it.

'At Good Earth, storytelling is not something that is done as an afterthought. We weave it into the creation of the product and there is no retrofitting. In fact, sometimes, the story leads to the product. Because this practice is seamlessly incorporated into the DNA of the brand, our voice and messaging are very authentic. Of course, there are people who follow us on social media because they want to buy our products, but we have a significant audience who are there for the storytelling on its own. In that sense, I suppose you can say that for us, content is a product. And when a brand has clear resonance, creating an online presence is easier. With each post, you set an expectation, so we also like to push the envelope and keep things exciting.

The most important advice I can offer is to make sure that the content creation team is well integrated within the organizational structure of a company. Often, companies place marketing, content and PR at the end of the chain and this is a big mistake. Having them involved from the start ensures that they understand the product journey and can articulate it much better. For anyone to communicate on behalf of the brand, they have to understand its soul. So, we work extremely closely with design and product development.

'At Good Earth we have always had the content team in-house—this is best for us because the way the brand works is very immersive and we like to have complete oversight on all aspects of brand communications. Our founder, Anita Lal, is also a natural storyteller and hence quite involved with this side of things. We don't follow trends, and nor do we chase perfection. Good Earth is, at the end of the day, a home-grown, organic brand that embraces a little bit of chaos and uncertainty. We have a very strong sense of provenance, and are India-proud, both of which really work in our favour. This is a very interesting fact because the messaging resonates quite seamlessly even with our NRI audiences.

'Secondly, please expand the lens on content. It is not just about three daily posts on Instagram. It has to include online customer service and marketing and sales communication. Especially in our new normal, when more people are shopping online. Members of your marketing and sales teams—whether on the shop floor or working on the website—have to know how to sell a product and talk to a luxury customer. Good Earth is very particular about making sure that everyone speaks the brand language.

'Today's customer wants authenticity and not a sharp sell. Brand values and ethics are very important decision makers, so they have to be baked into your storytelling. Otherwise, content is just a word and not a real function. At Good Earth, for example, our messaging pillars of hand-crafted, inspired by nature, and Indian luxury, all guide our storytelling

'In our online content, we focus a lot on design, colour, nature, history, wellness and lifestyle. Not only are these popular areas of interest, but they also fit into our brand DNA. There is a sharp visual aesthetic, in keeping with the fact that design is sacrosanct at Good Earth.

'We aim to create a feeling. In fact, our mandate is not to sell first. Every product needs a context in terms of styling, craft or how it can be used. We never ask people to buy something. We tell them a story of how this product can fit into their homes and lives. And then it's up to them to buy. Which is also why we are constantly creating a visual escape. There are a lot of quotes we share, and we are frequently nostalgic!

'During the lockdown necessitated by COVID 19 in 2020, for example, we created a series of artworks showing Delhi's monuments being taken over by real and mythical creatures. This was rooted in the reality of empty streets but also created a dream state, which felt very real to the brand.'

Are We Trending Yet?

We cannot talk about audiences without referencing social media. Likes, follows, engagement, and content are now building blocks of customer acquisition and retainment. I asked my friend Varun Rana, who has been a fashion editor, is a respected social commentator and now consults with brands on content and communication, to outline ten cardinal rules to help navigate social media.

1. **Be wise with your pennies**

Everything, including your seemingly 'free' social media, has a cost. It could be money, time, effort, or simply your bandwidth. Whatever kind of brand you happen to be—established, experimental, start-up—think of each of these outlets as an opportunity. Every opportunity, as we know, comes at the cost of another. So, see which platforms work for you and which don't. Avoid thinking in percentages, because every platform will work for you to some extent. This would divert your attention from those outlets that can actually give you better outcomes. For example, planning even small shoots and campaigns should be a targeted exercise, and those targets will be met when you are clear which platform they will be exposed on. Invest your time, effort, and money into specific platforms that will bring you the best results. Entire brands have been built solely on Instagram, with no presence on Pinterest, Reddit, Twitter, Quora, or Facebook. Choose your strategy, and go at it hammer and tongs.

2.   Think interdisciplinary and intersectional

These may be big-sounding words, but they have real-life applications and results that many brands are coming to appreciate of late. If you are talking about how sustainable your organic cotton kurtas are, your customers cannot be receiving them in plastic packaging when the order reaches their homes. If you profess gender equality, you cannot do it by numbers alone and must reach gender equity in how many men, women, and other genders are represented across your team hierarchy. If you want to be seen as a brand that supports its workers, get them all individual bank accounts, medical insurance, and PF benefits.

3.   Do it quietly

This brings us to a crucial point: avoid talking about whatever you're doing right as CSR. It is very tempting to make social and cultural correctness, inclusivity, and sustainability (in its many forms), and such agendas a part of your brand's talking points. This is folly. Think of these as the basics of your business and build on them internally. Doing the right thing should be normal, not an added bonus, or worse, a USP. As a business owner, you cannot be seen to be celebrating your ethical treatment of your staff and workers. It is the very least you can do. To then take the basics and shout about it from the rooftops of your social media channels shows bad taste. And the newly informed and sensitized consumer is immune to such gimmicks. Besides, they will lose no time on calling bullshit on such communication if it's something you're seen to be doing as a performance. You don't want to go there.

4. Be honest

Fashion, for example, is always a response to the zeitgeist—it chronicles the time in which it is created. So being sensitive to what is happening is a must. Some brands are known to allude to the ongoing social discourse as part of their work and vision and are not averse to taking a stance whether it's social, cultural, or even political. Good for them, but you don't have to be like them. In the current scenario, where your brand perception on social media may affect your bottom line, you may find yourself forced to engage in performative communication on topics like body issues, feminism, equality and equity, gender diversity, mental health, the global ecological crisis, sustainability, craft revival, etc.… If talking about any of these topics does not come naturally to you and is really not part of your work or your process, stay away in respectful silence and let others do the talking. Stick to the merits of your work and sell it through that.

5.   If you must, consult with experts

That said, there is no law anywhere that states that designers should not be speaking about global issues or commenting on the problems we see around us. Indeed, it is designers who are often deeply engrossed in the world they see around them, and that makes them stakeholders like any other human being. However, since a designer's work is tied to retail and profits, it becomes extremely important to not spread misinformation (even inadvertently) or co-opt/appropriate anyone's struggles as a means of propagating business. For example, anyone who isn't from the Dalit community wishing to speak about casteism would do well to consult with Dalit scholars and read the many works of Dr B.R. Ambedkar before creating any communication—visual or written—that may, once out in the public sphere, be harmful or insensitive to a cause that's real to so many citizens. There are hundreds of examples of brands that have fallen down such slippery slopes in the past, and everyone should learn from their mistakes.

6.   It's okay to not have a 'vision'

For too long a narrative existed that all great and successful brands start with a 'vision', whatever that may be. This is not true at all. This false fairy tale is often a retrofit achieved on social media because of the toxic nature of the platforms themselves. Nobody likes to admit that there was a time when they floundered, were unsure of where they are headed, or even considered shutting down entirely. On the flip side, the one great advantage of social media is that it has erased the difference between the leader and the consumer. Utilize this superpower to take your followers along on your journey from the very beginning. In doing so, you will create a community that is truly invested in your brand and feels connected to it, and therefore, your success.

7.   Everybody wants to be a thought leader

The speed of social media is a double-edged sword. It may help a brand grow super-fast, but it also creates a false narrative that equates business success with industry wisdom. To be known as a thought leader in any field, an individual needs to have invested considerable time working, learning, innovating, failing, experimenting, and constantly trying to do better. Thought leadership does not come from the ability to have useful thoughts because of mere experience: those are just your learnings, and you are welcome to share them with anyone on social media. True thought leadership comes from being able to discern, on a macro scale, what your chosen field requires, and the ability to express it in ways that will inspire others regardless of commercial and creative competition and business realities.

8.   F*** the media; own your content

Not all brands have the wherewithal to go all guns blazing in huge media-supported launches or campaigns. This is not a weakness or shortcoming at any level whatsoever. This simply means being creative. And as someone working in the creative field, this should ideally come easy to you. Refer back to Point 1 and see where best to utilize your limited budgets and how to create content that speaks to your audience. If you're consistent and have a unique point of view, the same media channels will cover your story in a few months or years without asking for a penny.

9. Expand your collaborations

Not all partnerships have to be design led. Collaborations are a way to exchange knowledge and bring in expertise. Think of unique ways of collaborating. Involve people from various fields: chefs, painters, poets, musicians, architects, lawyers, scientists, writers, street artists, students, institutions, a hundred others. This will diversify your own knowledge base and create unique opportunities for you to engage with a wider audience through your social media, which will also gain fresh content with each new, exciting partnership. Whatever you do, don't be boring.

10. Surround yourself with everything amazing

Whether it's the people you work with, the books you read, the social media handles you follow, the events you go to, your holidays, the humans you hang out with, the meals you cook/eat, the breaks you (should definitely) take—make each thing amazing. Not by putting in extra effort to live the Insta life and making it all look beautiful, but by ensuring that each aspect of your life and connections is constantly teaching you something new, interesting, surprising, and delightful. Instead of celebrities, follow museums, comedians, and scientists on Insta. Instead of going to fashion events, go to the Blind School Mela, or take homecooked food to an old-age home. Try to spend time with school and college students; they will surprise you endlessly (Bonus: you will realize that the future of the world is in good hands). Volunteer with your entire design team at the local dog shelter for a day of wagging tails and wet-licky kisses—pure therapy! This is important.

ON MY OWN

When you work by yourself—whether you call yourself a freelancer, a solopreneur, or just an individual hustling on your own—it can feel intimidating to handle all aspects of a brand, including storytelling, and retail. I asked my co-writer Chinmayee who is a solopreneur herself, and coaches people on how to run content and communications as a one-person show, to share her top tips:

1. 'Think of yourself as a business, not an individual and get as organised as you would be if you had a team. This means outlining all functions that need your time and attention, including your content and communication. Often, I find that my solopreneur clients will focus on finances or their supply chain but will wing it with their newsletters, social media and other collateral. Give your communication needs as much time and effort.

2. Choose your platforms wisely. Not everyone needs to be everywhere. Apply the same principles we have shared for brands – identify your audience, and meet them where they are.

3. Remember that quality always beats out quantity. If you work by yourself, it would be ridiculous to aim for five Instagram posts a week. Be very realistic and practical about how much time you can allocate to content creation. And, also, budget out your financial resources – images matter very much, and you will have to spend on them whether that means hiring a photographer, working with a graphic designer or buying memberships to photo libraries and editing apps.

4. Create a broad content calendar for each quarter, and a detailed one per month. And do this ahead of time. For example, by early March, you should have a calendar ready for the April to June quarter, with important dates and events marked out. As soon as you draw that up, create a monthly calendar that has every week's posting schedule for all the platforms and mediums you are on. Hot tip: build a bank of perennial content that can be reused.

5. Write your content and organise your imagery in advance. The worst thing to do is to be up on Tuesday night, trying frantically to put everything together to post on Wednesday morning. Remember that audiences appreciate consistency – it makes you look professional and dependable. I always like to have two weeks' worth of content ready to go at all times.

6. Repurpose as much as you can. Four Instagram posts can become a blog post, which can then be condensed into a newsletter. Marketing templates can be tweaked to create new ones. Don't reinvent the wheel all the time. Refresh older content and use it on different platforms. A post from two weeks ago can be made into a Story on Instagram with clever use of fonts and imagery.'

IN A NEW YORK MINUTE

There are few things better than working in Paris in your twenties. My first job at a PR agency called Herald Communications was just challenging enough but not too much so. I had a wonderful boss and mentor in Laurence, and despite the fact that I was not passionate about technology, I had worked hard on my beat and was doing a good job for my clients. But I knew I wanted much more. It surprises me how, even decades later, people will say to me, 'Why did you leave Paris? I would never have done that!' The truth is that Paris was not the place for me to grow in the way I hoped to.

I needed to be somewhere that would allow me to blend my French and Indian heritage, with a more global perspective. I also wanted to gain a much more diverse set of skills and expertise. Public relations at the time was different because you got a bird's-eye view of a domain or a brand—you never had a chance to sink your teeth in and gain more solid knowledge of it. I had a sense that this would not help me advance my career as I wanted to. This is a piece of advice I would offer any young person, regardless of what profession they are in: look at people a few years ahead of you, plot their journeys and consider if that trajectory will work for you. Adjust accordingly.

Another interesting thing I notice when I look back on that time is that the constant in my life has been a desire to expand my horizons by moving cities or countries. Uprooting yourself forces you to shift focus and change up your life and routine. It's not for everyone, but it has been my way of getting out of a comfort zone and upping my ambition and skillset—growth is not a linear process for any of us.

While working in Paris, I had made a couple of work trips to New York. The city's energy, sense of possibility and unabashed ambition drew me in, as it does millions of others. My eventual move there was pure happenstance, perhaps fuelled by my deep desire for it. A chance meeting with the scion of a family-run hospitality business led to me being hired to head communications for them at their headquarters in New York. The big move, when it happened, did not just take me from one city to the next, it also gave me a chance to move from working for a client to being a client myself.

The business I now worked for included hotels and restaurants, film production, and public affairs, and as their head of communications, I was in charge of managing five to six PR firms spread across the US and Europe to represent all the properties of the group. What made it possible for me to find my feet was the fact that my time in Paris had trained me in how agencies work. So now, as a client, I knew what to expect and what not to settle for.

The filters I had for Paris professionally did not work in New York. I had to read the pulse of the city, decode its culture, and tap into that particular moment in time. And New York is the best city in the world in which to learn how to be a consummate professional.

People are punctual, all about business, and they respect one another's commitment and expertise. Hierarchy and bureaucracy, which define so much of how work is done in France, were not relevant in New York, which values people who get the job done. My long work lunches with two glasses of wine in Paris were quickly replaced with power meetings that lasted less than an hour as we picked on bowls of salad. Conversations were more focused and to the point—you had to show up being your best and make space for others to do the same. All the practices I now nag my team to follow—systems and processes, agendas and recaps, time management and client relations—I learnt from a range of people and firms between Paris and New York and built on them over the years. I learnt to deep dive into a brand, and because I had a stake in branding or PR decisions, I saw the benefits of an in-house function. Besides, it was enormous fun to be on the client side in meetings. I also realized that hospitality is the best training to learn how to 'be of service', build a rapport, genuinely care about keeping a client happy, and provide a unique experience.

Of course, moving cities and switching careers were not easy or smooth sailing—I don't want this to feel like a 'and just like that' moment at all. Working in a family business for the first time, I had to learn to gauge and interpret everyone's opinions and interpersonal equations and apply the information while being a professional catalyst for the team. Years on, I find this to be a useful skill, since India is still a country of family businesses, and in dealings with clients I can always understand each member's role and contribution.

New York also pushed my professional buttons in a completely different way—it is an assertive, confident city, and you have to learn to network seamlessly. My employers were fantastic at building and growing connections across the board, and I had to learn—fast—to get over my inherent shyness to catch up with them.

As the head of communications at a company that was built by self-made immigrants, I was occupying a unique space at the time, and perhaps the enormity of it was only made clear to me in hindsight. I had to use my voice with conviction and be very open-minded but also deal with opposition and disagreement in a healthy way. The thing about public relations as a career is that it does not demand a specific academic qualification, but what it does require of you is to string all your personal and professional experiences together and adapt them to every situation. It teaches you to gravitate towards people who are not like you and create a space in which you both can have a constructive conversation.

Working with the family was a lesson in building relationships and a successful business in a pre-digital era. They were masterful in the way they strategically cultivated a network. Social media and digital connectivity have made it relatively easy to make friends and influence people, as it were. The world is also more diverse now, though far from what it should be. At that time, my employers and myself were often the only people of colour at a benefit or fundraiser, and my boss was usually the host. I cannot emphasize how unusual this was and how hard he had worked to get there.

Above all else, though, what I learnt from the company culture was to truly love what you do. Not in the Pinterest-image manner, but in a deeper, more meaningful way. I realized that I had to stay passionately interested in my professional life and committed to letting it and myself evolve. I could say that working in New York was a dream come true and leave it at that because, in many ways, it was. The people I represented loved publicity, visibility, and coverage. I had the privilege of managing several agencies and meeting journalists and tastemakers on both coasts of the US, from England, and from India. I suppose these days, I could sum all this up as #blessed, but there was also a #hustle aspect to it, which caught up with me eventually. Weekends blurred into weekdays and I was always on call, 24/7. Because the scope of my work and what my clients dabbled in was so vast, I began to feel a little bit like I was on a carousel that did not stop.

There will always be challenges to any job, and days you really don't want to have anything to do with it. And it must never replace or completely swallow up your personal life, which is why boundaries are important.

As much as I loved the fact that I now had an incredible depth of knowledge about the hospitality industry, and to some extent, public affairs, I began to itch for independence and the freedom to work on my own.

I feel like the entrepreneurial bug was in the air in New York at that point in time, and I caught it. Here, I have to add that I had moved to the US not with the American dream in mind, but with the Indian dream in mind. As much as I wanted to be in New York, doing what I did, my goal had always been to work with Indian brands and, eventually, be in India. My desire to connect more deeply with India intersected perfectly with the white space I identified in the large Indian diaspora market—there were huge numbers of Indian and Indian-origin people who were served by focused publications and TV channels. This diaspora was very influential in terms of politics and as consumers, but there was a gap to be filled by a public relations agency that acted as a bridge between all the stakeholders.

The idea grew into Peepul PR, which I started with two friends in April 2006. I made the decision to do this with partners as I was lucky to connect with like-minded professionals who had an adventurous spirit, like me. Some people work better on their own from the start, but I needed a sounding board and an ally as I set off on a really daunting journey with my own company. And then there's also the matter of renting a space or working from home—we were very prudent with how we structured the business right at the start. We set up a small office off 9th and Broadway and decided to pay ourselves salaries, but kept them small so the pressure was off a little bit.

I also made a personal decision which I have never regretted and it taught me something I still value—I decided to take a bank loan to give myself a little cushion as I quit a very coveted job. At this point in my career, I had not put away enough savings and I did not want to waste time or energy on regret and fear. Taking a loan was my way of investing in myself, and it gave me a true sense of security. I did not have to sacrifice too much and could focus on the work we had ahead of us. This is a piece of advice I still give anyone who will listen to me.

Don't ever start a new venture with anxiety about money. As long as you are being prudent, borrowing some funds from family or a bank will act as a solid bridge to your future.

People's advice on every aspect of starting a business will vary. I can only share what worked for me. Whether you should do this by yourself or with one or more partners; renting an office space versus working from home; how much to invest back in the business versus what you pay yourself— each one of these is a valid concern. For myself, I knew that I wanted to take care of myself first. It's like the emergency statement on a flight: put that oxygen mask on yourself first before you can help others. If I was not feeling secure and confident in my future, I could not possibly do my best work.

Our first client was the designer Payal Singhal, who would eventually become a close friend and someone who later helped me find my feet in Mumbai. We also signed up to represent the respected Indian gallery Bodhi Art, and Cobra Beer, helping organize events and interactions with the press. Because we had created a niche for ourselves and were catering to an audience that really needed our services, doors opened for us that might not have. I began to meet stalwarts like Anand Mahindra and Subhash Chandra, which was incredible and validated my belief in what we were doing.

In particular, I still remember our experience with ICICI Bank, who reached out to us to represent them. We were honest in letting them know that while we had no experience working with clients in the financial sector, we did have an excellent network, which we would use to do our best. What ICICI did was very clever and gave us a huge boost—they hired a PR agency that focused on finance, but also gave us a mandate to communicate their launch to the Indian diaspora audience. This truly validated our values and our expertise. The late Charudutt Deshpande took that chance on us and he became a true mentor to me, later giving me a project as I made the move from New York to Mumbai.

Those early years of running a business were an education. I learnt how to decode a culture and suss out the potential of an industry. As a publicist and now an entrepreneur, I could not work in a silo. While I always enjoyed networking and meeting new people, it was now a necessity. I had to develop the ability to identify the people and brands to know, because my clients depended on me to bring them that information.

My time in New York was all about reinvention, personally and professionally. I had taken a leap of faith, leaving Paris and everything I knew, to come to a new city and redefine success and ambition for myself. Even today, neither of these concepts are linear for me. And then I took another massive gamble by founding Peepul. Decades later, as I write this, I realize that I have periodically pushed myself out of my comfort zone by moving cities or countries or taking chancy professional decisions, and it has worked well. It's never easy, but I don't think it's meant to be.

Finally, I was filled with gratitude for everyone who gave us a chance, or a second chance. It is never easy trying to find your feet in a city as competitive as New York, and at the time, PR was a high-powered profession filled with people who were at the top of their game. Everyone who took a meeting with me signed Peepul up to tell their story and offered me counsel. This just reaffirmed my faith in myself. So perhaps the biggest lesson I learnt was to also always give people a chance when they deserve it.

2

What's
the BIG
idea?

CHAPTER FIVE

Finding Your Bearings

Before I get really granular and help you understand whether you need a PR agency, a solo publicist, and/or an in-house publicity department, I want to take a minute to address two major topics that I don't think get enough emphasis. One is understanding your customer as best as you can. And the second is scoping out the media landscape. Why do these matter before you get down and dirty with PR? Because without this information under your belt, you are not going to be able to focus and see results.

KNOW THY CUSTOMER

Remember what Seth Godin said about the connection economy? Nothing highlights his idea more than the fact that the customer/consumer/client is more powerful than ever. If you don't know who your target audience is, you could get lost very, very quickly.

The number one reason for this is our hyper-connected, social media-centric, digital reality. Think back to just ten years ago: your primary interaction with a brand was in real life, at a store or an event. You were introduced to it via advertising, grew a connection through traditional media (print, digital, or television), and then built a tangible relationship IRL. Now, you need never step into a store if you don't want to, because you can choose to build a relationship entirely online. The touchpoints of that relationship have multiplied, and geography no longer matters. I could be on vacation in Kerala and buy a dress off MatchesFashion because I had a whim to. And what a brand stands for is now a key driver in winning over customer loyalty. People want to know which side of the fence you are on, no matter what that fence represents—politics, ethics, or philosophy, among other things. Being aware of and nimble around sociocultural realities is essential because conversations change in a matter of hours (sometimes, minutes) and you have to be able to gauge what is expected of you to stay relevant. And sometimes, what is expected of you is to do and say nothing.

All of this underlines the need for a brand to know who their customer is. But how do you get there?

The first thing I advise a founder or a founding team to do is identify people within their own personal and professional worlds who they see as ideal customers and talk to them in depth about what they believe in, what their needs and expectations are, and how they consume and share information. If you have a tangible product, have them sample it, and get their thoughts on everything from the packaging to whether you are able to deliver on the promise made. In case what you are launching is a service, do a dry run if possible with them. Even if you have a focus group of ten or fifteen people, their feedback will be invaluable to you.

The second way to go is to study your competition, understand who their customer base is and find a way to tap into it. Using social media, can you reach out to a focus group and request them to take a survey and/ or try your product or service? Or you can choose to do a soft launch on

Instagram, for example, and using content cleverly, see who is drawn to you organically.

Finally, I am also a big fan of recommending pop-ups and exhibitions if you have a product that is conducive to that model. Being in a physical space gives you so many advantages—you can converse with people directly and answer questions, identify what they are drawn to and what might not appeal to them, and scope out the competition.

And once you know who your customer is, you will know how best to converse with them. For instance, there are brands who maintain a social media presence but communicate with their customer via WhatsApp, and do very well. They may not even engage in PR activities. Their primary connection with their customers is via exhibitions, and they build those relationships the old-fashioned way. On the other hand, a lot of brands that target millennials/Gen Z focus first on Instagram as a way to connect with their audience. They might also choose to associate with or organize music festivals, which are a big draw, especially with the younger consumer.

TALKING ABOUT A (MEDIA) REVOLUTION

All industries have been reshaped by COVID-19 to a varying degree, but in India, I find that traditional media has been, perhaps, one that has been impacted and changed quite indelibly. At the same time, social and digital media have grown enormously in influence and power. What PR does via traditional media is help you talk to all your stakeholders, and social media helps you build a direct line of communication, especially with your customers.

Sujata Assomull, founding editor of *Harper's Bazaar India* and a prolific fashion writer, emphasizes the key difference between social and traditional media. In the former, you are speaking for yourself, but in the case of the latter, someone else is speaking for you, which can sometimes be much more valuable, 'A publication, especially a legacy publication is known for its edit, or its point of view. A person reads that publication as it knows that publication has done its checks and balances. It gives that third party seal of approval—and that is an endorsement money can't buy,' she says.

You need both medias and they have to be in sync with one another so you have a seamless universe of communication. One does not replace the other, even though these days I find that a lot of brands think they can swap one out for the next. Focusing only on social media works if you know that this is the best way to talk to your target audience. As is the case for Le Mill, the Mumbai-based multi-designer store founded and run by Cecilia Morelli Parikh and Julie Leymarie. They find that their energy and resources are best spent talking to their clients directly.

'We see ourselves as merchants whose job is to cull the best from everywhere and bring it to our community in Mumbai. We knew, early on, that customer service would be a cornerstone of our brand, and we started to develop products catering to this. Our personal shopping and at-home shopping experience were firsts in the country, and proved very successful. We always see ourselves and tell our staff that we want to be friends to our clients. In the first five years of Le Mill, our goal was to win loyal customers. And Instagram helped us do this, by opening up borders in a way nothing else could. It was also a key way for us to build out our brand aesthetically, which we did with amazing collaborators, creating a visual language for Le Mill that we could broadcast over social media. Instagram is also an amazing way for customers in India to stay up-to-date on trends,' says Cecilia.

At Peepul, we spent 2020 studying and pivoting to the new world order, while building on our past experiences and learnings. And here are the key lessons we found, which I will expand on in the coming chapters:

1. The fundamental difference between traditional and social media, from a communications viewpoint, is who controls the narrative. On your own social media channels, you do. And in a magazine, the editor and writer do. Both are valuable and every brand can do with a healthy mix of traditional and social media (we recommend a 40:60 ratio).

2. Social media is definitely more authentic and serves as a direct line of communication, which is powerful. But it has to be handled just right.

3. Building a network within the right traditional media outlets can prove to be extremely beneficial. While you might feel that a customer's endorsement on social media is fantastic and an influencer's post is pure gold, the truth is that the clear, authoritative, and informed opinion of a respected editor or writer adds much-needed heft to your brand narrative.

4. Whatever it is you choose to do, you have to stay true to your brand values, fine-tune to the frequency of your target audience, and be very clear on what your goal is with that activity or messaging.

5. Change is now a constant both in traditional and social media, so staying nimble is very, very important.

My peer and friend, Pareina Thapar, who worked as a journalist for years before co-founding Longform India, represents some of the most compelling brands in India. I asked her for her thoughts on the new world of communications.

'In the traditional landscape, everyone understood the functions of advertising agencies, PR agencies, media planning advisories, sales and marketing functions, etc.—there were defined boundaries. In social media, newer forms of roles have emerged and are ever-changing. For those who don't understand the medium enough, it can be overwhelming to understand and navigate different functions. E-commerce versus social media, storytelling and content strategy versus performance marketing—it is never-ending,' she said. 'But the main focus is unification of brand voice [and goals] across all platforms. For instance, in-store experience and customer service may be superb in the offline world for one brand but it may have a terrible digital curation and brand messaging. On the other hand, a brand can be very good-looking digitally and off the mark in the real world. Being good on omni channels is becoming essential to the survival of brands. There is no balance.

'When you work on a brand's identity and storytelling, you have to be able to live in the past, present, and future all at the same time. Trends come and go and are definitely important because they keep you in the now. Learnings from the past help you recognize what is cyclical, learning to be future forward is important for your evolution. Being curious and having an appetite to observe and absorb is important, and this takes discipline to build. You also need to be nimble and quick on the uptake.

'As a cohesive communications strategy advisor, I believe it's important to know why you want to work with a brand as much as you should ask why they want to work with you. And don't be afraid to say no to anything that hampers your long-term growth—there is a power to that, and it saves you time and energy. This also means that you need to know what your skills are and if you are not competent in a certain aspect of business, either focus on what you are good at or invest in people who complement you. Or just spend time educating yourself.

'Storytelling for brands is all about listening, observing, and staying interested in the world around you. Passion, purpose, and drive are very important. Don't get caught up in the noise around you and focus on the key areas that require your attention.'

To get the other side of the story, I spoke with Mehernaaz Dhody, editor-in-chief of *Grazia India*, who has decades of experience working in Indian fashion magazines. 'Storytelling has to be authentic and not for the sake of marketing. Don't mimic another brand's strategy and use your storytelling to highlight your own selling points. Build a tribe that resonates with your brand – it could be your clientele, or your supporters in the media. Don't just pick the influencer or platform with the highest numbers,' she said. 'A successful brand offers not just a great product and/or service, but also great communication. And it does help if you believe in following sustainable (and honest) practices.'

Mehernaaz also advises brands to, 'Invest in your assets and make sure your communication (and customer experience, if applicable) is precise and meaningful. Be transparent about your marketing strategy. It does not work to offer your exclusives to one media brand and leftovers to another. Finally, don't try to push one media house to use a particular piece of content editorially and pay for another to publish the same content. It really negates the whole exercise.'

CHAPTER SIX

What Does PR Actually Mean?

A rather cheesy way of describing public relations is to say that 'advertising is what you pay for, publicity is what you pray for'. (I did not say this. Helen Woodward, who was the first female advertising executive in the US, said it in 1938. Some things clearly never change.) Given my own screwball sense of humour, I quite like this definition but, of course, PR is now so much more multi-faceted and holistic.

We live in the age of social media, when anyone can post a picture of a new product to Instagram, review a restaurant or spa on Twitter, and offer opinions on anything at all on a range of similar platforms. So it can be easy to think that PR in its classical sense is outdated and/or irrelevant. But as my friend and founding editor-in-chief of *Vogue* India, Priya Tanna, says, 'I think we often forget the role of public relations. We mistake it for press-release journalism. But it's much deeper than that. In the post-truth and fake news age, where 280 characters and less can make or break a brand, I think PR is more relevant than ever. The role of PR is to remind a brand to know itself, to adapt when needed, and to help create, guide, and communicate your brand to the outside world. A strong PR outfit can also easily double up as a potent business development agency.'

At its best, public relations is a strategic communication process to share authentic storytelling which builds mutually beneficial relationships between organisations, individuals, and their target audience. I think of it as the business of information and relationships. A publicist's key responsibility is to help raise awareness and build a DNA and legacy for a brand by positioning it perfectly both in the market and in the minds of its consumers. These are the aspects of the job that I can tell you have not changed from my first day on the job more than two decades ago. What I have added to my KRA today is to strengthen community relations, since social media and the digital universe are now such important factors to consider. My team and I work hard to help shape content creation on the brand's channels and look at influencer marketing as well, because a publicist's job is to help a brand build credibility and trust and ensure that the right stories are being shared on all channels. Every brand has an identity and wants to be perceived a certain way to connect with and grow its target audience. And a publicist or agency is the curator of that information.

When I look back through the lens of cities and countries I have worked in, it is very clear that while, public relations has a set of clear functions and purposes, every market uniquely shapes its own industry. To get a better perspective and wider context to PR in India, I chatted with Archana Jain, a consummate publicist who founded and manages PR Pundit, which is one of India's leading and respected agencies.

'Every six to seven years, we have seen an evolution in the media landscape and also of PR in India. The 1990s was when business journalism came of age. With the advent of CNBC TV-18 in 1999, business television added a new dimension to our profession. Digital media emerged on the scene in 2010; social media (and influencers) in 2015; and we are flirting with podcasts since 2020.

'Global lifestyle brands began to think of India as a market in 2005. Many of them were testing waters and therefore engaged with the market through distribution partners. In the PR business too, we were engaged with the global brands mostly through their India distribution partners. There were exceptions like Moët Hennessy and Swarovski that had taken an early plunge and set up direct operations already. Luxury lifestyle PR started taking shape in 2007-08 when luxury brands like Gucci, Tod's, Estée Lauder, and magazines like *Vogue* arrived on the Indian shores.

'Integrated communication solutions came to be expected from PR firms with the arrival of global brands. Being a publicist today is no longer about inviting media or making extensive guest lists. It is about creating multiple circles of influences for the brand. We have to get customers acquainted with the brand for them to consider buying it. PR firms are now not only expected to manage press and influencer communications but also recommend creative formats of engagement with consumers, foster marketing and communication collaborations, offer influencer marketing solutions and have the capabilities to manage owned social media platforms to tell the brand, product and service story, etc.'

EVERYONE NEEDS PR!

Not just brands, everyone needs publicity
and the right publicity!

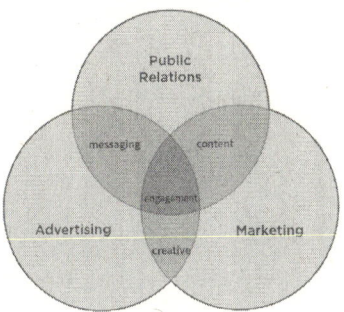

Public Relations is not just for brands, big or small, it is for individuals
too because individuals create brand and people connect to other people
and they consume brands.

Take me or our firm for example, this is not just a knowledge session,
it also becomes a publicity tactic, so more people know through my
experience what my firm foes, the kind of expertise it has and may be
give us their business.

PR is not just about building a narrative, it is about consistently telling
a story that resonates with your audience and makes them trust you.

TRUST is the OPERATIVE WORD

GOOD PR OR BAD PR CAN MAKE
OR BREAK A COMPANY

WHAT IS PUBLIC RELATIONS?

WHAT PEOPLE THINK WE DO   WHAT WE ACTUALLY DO

HOW HAS PR CHANGED?

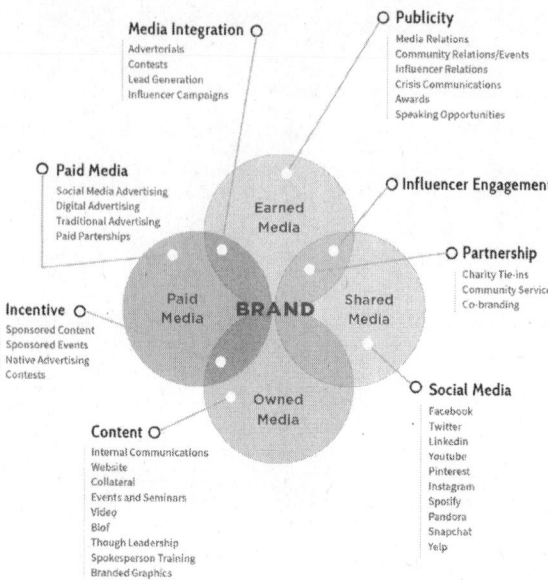

Media Integration
Advertorials
Contests
Lead Generation
Influencer Campaigns

Publicity
Media Relations
Community Relations/Events
Influencer Relations
Crisis Communications
Awards
Speaking Opportunities

Paid Media
Social Media Advertising
Digital Advertising
Traditional Advertising
Paid Partnerships

Influencer Engagement

Partnership
Charity Tie-ins
Community Service
Co-branding

Incentive
Sponsored Content
Sponsored Events
Native Advertising
Contests

Social Media
Facebook
Twitter
Linkedin
Youtube
Pinterest
Instagram
Spotify
Pandora
Snapchat
Yelp

Content
Internal Communications
Website
Collateral
Events and Seminars
Video
Blof
Though Leadership
Spokesperson Training
Branded Graphics

Earned Media · Paid Media · BRAND · Shared Media · Owned Media

---

CONSISTENT STORYTELLING AND IMAGERY

Listening
To employees, trusted
associated and your
consumer

Building Narratives
Create a handbook of words,
phrases that depict you,
key words and anecdotes
that are unique to you etc.

**Consistent
Communication**
Build templates and writing
styles that are consistent
and connect to a brand's
personality. Centre your
PR plan around your
marketing calender.

**Constantly Identifying
Newer Audiences**
Everyday you will find a new
audience and you everyday
you need to identify this new
person or entity and find a way
to approach them and seed
your brand. Your TG has to
constantly evolve

Being Fearless
Have an inner circle.
Do not get intimidated by
feedback that comes to you
from outside this group

Attempting the Audacious

To talk about the evolution of PR, and how to build a successful agency, I turned to Dilip Cherian, the legendary image guru, who co-founded Perfect Relations, south Asia's largest image management and public affairs company. (In 2016, the firm was acquired by Dentsu Aegis.) Dilip is a man who has shaped the Indian PR landscape, and I am going to let him tell the story in his inimitable way.

'Founding Perfect Relations was the result of a conversation at a friend's house. He had put me in touch with the CEO of Pepsico India, who was using a global agency at the time and he was really bothered by the fact that they were charging by the hour, which led to a complicated billing process. My friend said to me, "Why can't you do this?" I thought he was quite mad but he was actually very serious. I was running a newspaper at the time and when I met the head of Pepsico, he said, "I will give this account to you because you are a business journalist and you understand all of this. I have confidence in you." There was no pitch, and no plan. I spoke to my colleague, Bobby Kewalramani and we started Perfect Relations with a motorcycle and no office.

'So building scale is really about attempting the audacious. We sub-leased the drawing room of a Member of Parliament to use as an office. It was right next to Rashtrapati Bhavan and Bobby would speed off on his bike to distribute press releases at ITO where all the media offices are. There was a phone booth close to our little office that we used to make all calls. We had no idea what we were doing, but I tell people now that all you need are competence and capability. I had spent a decade as a reporter first, and then an assistant editor. I had been the editor of *Business India*, and helped set up another newspaper called *The Observer* for Dhirubhai Ambani. (You really understood public policy and business when you spent time with him.) My skills of research and writing came from my days as a journalist. Growing a publicity business involves working endless hours, being consistent and building a depth of knowledge. A fancy degree does not qualify you for PR. These traits do.

'PR is still very much about column centimeters and mentions in the press, while also being about data mining, AI and machine learning. But at the end of the day, whatever fancy algorithms you use, the client usually says, "I want to see what you've done for me. Have you got me a piece in *The Economist*? Do I have a meeting with a joint secretary in the Ministry of IT because of a thoughtful piece you placed for me in *The Hindu*, which is a newspaper that secretary reads?"

'The bottomline is—if you cut out the fanciful cloak of respectability, PR is about what you have delivered to your clients that day. A corporate communications executive will count clips but it is also about the right headlines and the position that the coverage places the company in. When I am hiring someone, I don't want to know how many clients they can bring in or if they are interested in working on strategy. (Also, I want to add that no one is qualified to talk strategy until they have at least 20 years of experience.) I always ask a prospective hire if they can write a press release in under 20 minutes and make sure it is error-free. Will it contain a phrase that can become a hashtag? Or will it have enough impact for PTI and Reuters to carry it? They need to have the humility to respect the client's experience.

'Finally, as an agency or a publicist, it is important to be ahead of the curve. At Perfect Relations, we started prioritising social media eight years ago and investing in it. Now, 50 per cent of our team is purely digital. We explain to clients why it is important for them to invest in social media and strategize with them. The only problem is that social media needs revisiting more often than traditional media. Even the biggest hit on Twitter or Instagram only lasts an hour or two. You need to constantly bounce back, shaved and showered. And it is not cheap and cheerful. Great content requires money and you need to spend on promoting it.'

CHAPTER SEVEN

Introducing Your Brand to the World

Now that you know who your customer is, choosing how to navigate media, communications, and publicity is your next big decision. I will be the first to say that not every brand needs a PR agency to get their job done. I know it might sound odd coming from me, but the truth is that several brands can communicate with their customer very effectively on their own and don't need a partner to introduce them to magazines or newspapers. This is often because their customer focuses on social media or because they have built a base that engages with them directly and profitably. Or perhaps the decision is driven by the fact that their resources are best spent on handling their PR in-house.

While PR is a branding and awareness tool, I see it also as a catalyst for business, especially in India. The (uncomfortable) truth is that the media in the luxury and lifestyle space is not as powerful in India anymore as it was or still is in the US or UK. And neither are publicists. Some of the larger agencies and successful independent publicists are powerhouses on their own merit, and are boosted by their client list. India has a different reality, so if an agency just has coverage or mentions to show for itself, there is no incentive or value to clients investing in having one on board. I firmly believe that as a business, we are to blame if publicists are seen as dispensable. The only way to avoid this is to stay nimble and ahead of the game. If an agency does not keep up, it loses out. Which is why I always sleep with one eye open, and the best of my peers do too.

PICKING A SIDE

Let's break this down. Why do you need a publicist, in whatever shape and form? Because you will benefit from having a person or team who believes in your brand and vision, will champion both, and be your eyes and ears, helping you constantly finetune your business.

Anita Dongre, designer and founder of the iconic eponymous brand, says, 'A publicist comes in as a bridge between the media, the world, and you. If they are good at what they do, they offer strategy and become a key sounding board. [At a brand] we spend all our time looking inwards, and a publicist can help you see what you cannot see on your own.'

The ideal publicist—whether at an agency or working in-house—has the ability to read people and trends, tapping into the zeitgeist to build a connection between the brand and the market. They will be able to help you decipher reactions to your product/service and offer feedback that is (and always should be) productive and proactive so you can build better versions of what you do. Of course, they help you build a network of allies in the media and with influencers on social media so you are supported and boosted by the right people. Where relevant and possible, they also build your profile in the market to bring gravitas to the brand.

To make this easy for you, I've shortlisted the questions an entrepreneur or team need to ask themselves before they pick a side:

- What is your fundamental vision for public relations in the context of your brand? Some companies see it as an essential function because they need it to communicate effectively with their target audience, to tell a really well-crafted story, or to hone their profile in the business. Others—and I have found this is particularly true for brands in the B2B space—may find that it is just not something they have to invest in.

- Do you need someone to work with you month after month for an extended period of time, such as a year or two? Or would it serve you better to bring people in for projects and/or as consultants?

- How wide a network do you need to help you get to your goal? Will you able to build it with an in-house team?

- Finally, how much of your budget can you spare for this function? And where will it be best spent—on creating an in-house department or bringing an agency on board?

HIRING AN AGENCY

Hiring an agency, to me, can be determined by one primary point: do you need a group of people who are on your side and bring to the table what you and your team are missing? By bringing the right agency on board, you will benefit from multiple sets of relationships and their insider status in the market.

Between us, my team and I have a wide network that extends to different industries and markets. We know what editors, influencers, and changemakers are thinking about because we are in constant touch with them. And because we have built these relationships over years, they will be more honest and upfront with us than they would with a brand founder or team. Our clients gain from our access to editorial calendars and insider conversations, which we can distil for them as and when required. And because we represent a cluster of brands and individuals, we have more bargaining power that we bring into play.

Anita Lal of Good Earth, who is a client of ours at Peepul, says she benefits from working with an agency because 'I see a publicist as our connecting window to the world in order to collaborate with others and also get a feel of the current landscape.'

When you are shortlisting agencies, look at their experience and expertise in your industry. How much interest do they have in your brand? Do you see them as potential champions for your product or service? Can you see them pitching and selling your brand to the right people? And please spend time thinking about the size of the agency, too. If you have an established brand that needs a lot of attention, a boutique agency with a small team might not be the solution, even if they are keen and the budget is easier to manage. Another question that clients often overlook is whether they need an agency with a national (or even international) network and not one that might be city- or region-specific. My biggest piece of advice is to not scrimp on the research and consideration that you do before you approach anyone.

Finally, if you have different verticals or sub-brands, it is completely acceptable to hire two or more agencies as long as there is no overlap between what they do.

Making It Work

Deepika Prabhu is one of my partners at Peepul, and has vast experience working both in marketing and in PR. I asked her to write about the most essential rules to finding the right agency and building a productive relationship.

'The first and most important thing I have to say is that PR is primarily an awareness tool, not a sales tool. So as an agency, Peepul positions itself as an advisory and branding partner. For an agency, nothing is more daunting than over-messaging or working with celebrity-focused brands because what can we do to create multiple avenues of storytelling and communication? Not very much. So, the second essential point I want to make before we look at how to work with an agency is that not everyone needs to. Just because your friend has a publicist, you don't need one too. Think very clearly about what your goals are and if you need an agency to help you accomplish them, or if you can handle it in-house or on your own. For example, some global brands identify their key touchpoints for the year and work with PR agencies only for those, while handling the rest of their publicity needs in-house.

'Next, figure out what kind of agency you want. To get the best results out of the collaboration, you need to be very clear about three things, in my opinion. One, what is the scope of work? If you expect a boutique agency to work on everything from documents to media relations to coverage to event, that is a big ask and they may need more time than you have. What is the expectation from the PR agency in terms of results? A lot of people are not clear about why they hire an agency, and this can lead to a lot of confusion. Either be specific in terms of coverage, and influencer outreach, or focus on intangibles like building media relationships. Finally, do you want a courier service that will just deliver all of your press materials? Or do you want an agency or publicist with opinions that they are not afraid to share? There is no right answer. All I am saying is—be very clear so you find the right partner.

'The final piece of the puzzle is deciding when to bring an agency on board. This can feel a bit overwhelming and it varies from brand to brand. The ideal thing to do is to determine what the first big goal is. If it is a launch, think backwards—how much time will an agency need to accomplish everything before the big day? Especially if you don't have the capacity in-house to work on a bio, press materials, social media strategy, media relations, influencer outreach, etc., you might want to get your agency on board months ahead of time. If your goal is brand building, you might want to have your publicist or agency on board right at the start because they will be able to contribute meaningfully.

'Once you engage with an agency or publicist, spend time getting to know one another. At Peepul, we like to spend a month, more or less, to get to know a new client and draw up an effective, strategic plan. At the end of this time, our goal is to create a messaging matrix, PR plan and press materials, and have a very clear road map of what we're going to focus on. First, we define pillars—this is what my brand stands for, this is what my product is, and this is the route in which I sell (e-commerce/brick and mortar retail, etc). Under each one, we add objectives and key messages.

'One of our first questions to potential or new clients is—what is the scale and reach of your product and not everyone is able to answer it fully. A lot of Indian brands call themselves luxury while they are masstige or premium. It's not so much about the price points but actually about the values your product represents. Think about that very carefully. Think about your niche this way to make it easier:

- Who is your customer?
- How many people do you want to sell to?
- Where do you want to retail?
- What do you want to achieve with the storytelling, online and offline?

More often than not, brands tend to describe themselves in comparison to another brand in the market. Or they offer one-word descriptors and don't take as much of a deep dive into knowing their consumer, and understanding the positioning. For example, most luxury brands that come to me talk about craftsmanship but at this point, that is just brand hygiene. It is not an origin story. Dig deeper, be more compelling and come up with something really original and convincing. Every brand has it in them. You just have to do the work to bring that story to life.

'An example I can share is of a former client, Original Madras Trading Company, a family-owned business that sells men's shirts and trousers created on looms. Their signature print is madras checks. Their USP is that they make the fabric, and design and manufacture the shirt but sell through international multi-brand stores. When they came to us, their objective was clear—they wanted to be seen as purveyors of original Madras checks.

'The product objective was to emphasise that these shirts never go out of style and they have a sense of humour to them. The retail objective was to be in the coolest concept stores in the world. We then defined the messaging points for the brand and the founder which included the origin story of how the company started off by making the fabric only, and we wanted to talk about their sustainability initiatives as well as how to style their products. How you action this differs slightly from brand to brand. For OMTC, we suggested having a brand manifesto that clearly said, these are our five values and this is how we uphold them. Because the brand story was a deep dive, a simple boilerplate did not do the job well.

'The reason I talk about this brand is that they were very generous in their conversations and exchanges with us. The more you share with your publicist, the better they can do their job. I know Srimoyi says this too, multiple times. If you are not transparent with your PR partners, they cannot help you.'

THE DIY OPTION

Picking an in-house publicist is almost like choosing a partner—you have to be in sync, challenge one another, and be able to have dinner together a couple of times a week.

The first thing to look for in a potential publicist, apart from their knowledge, network, and experience, is whether they can tune into your vision and goals for your brand. I would also look for emotional intelligence and the potential to push the envelope—you will only be able to verify these once you work together, but seeing a spark is important.

It goes without saying that you need someone who understands the art and science of PR, but they also need to know how to apply these to your particular industry. Do not be afraid to ask them straight out if they have a strong network of relationships that can be leveraged for you. One of my usual interview questions is, 'Name five key contacts on your speed dial.'

And if you are a start-up brand, do not hire someone with less experience than you. As a young publicist in New York, I once worked for a new brand and it just did not go well at all.

Given the complex and multifaceted nature of communications right now, I would highly recommend you merge functions, especially if you do not have generous budgets. PR melds well with social media, sales, and marketing, and you can divide and conquer based on what your calendar looks like. Or bring in interns and/or consultants to chip in during busy seasons.

I always recommend the DIY approach to F&B and hospitality brands because the nature of their business demands that they have someone paying attention round the clock to publicity. And this sounds counterintuitive, but a niche fashion, beauty, or lifestyle brand will benefit from this too, because they can combine different communication, sales, and marketing roles into one or two quite successfully.

Peter D'Ascoli, who is the founder of D'Ascoli, a niche luxury fashion and textiles brand, has always kept these functions in-house. I asked him what drives that. He said, 'The decision to create the design and marketing materials in-house stems from two inputs—practicality and experience. It is a simple lack of funding that causes us to create everything in-house, but we know that, constrained by finances or not, this is something that we must do. Through experience we know that our design and marketing vision must emanate from within us and not from without.

'We can and sometimes do avail ourselves of outside talent but, in order to be authentic, to bring an authentic voice to the market, this vision must come from only us. We must define ourselves, and senior management must constantly fight to maintain control of our brand image in the ever-evolving marketplace. For example, the short-term success of a design or product should not necessarily dictate the direction the company should take. Allowing market conditions, sales, and distribution to drive future design and marketing decisions by themselves is analogous to a rudderless ship being blown about by a changing wind.'

Stay Agile, Be Strategic

I requested Pranay Baidya, a talented designer with his own atelier, to share practical tips about running a business by himself, and juggling all aspects of it. Pranay is like family to me, and someone I respect for the manner in which he has built a brand, and for how professionally and efficiently he runs it.

'Having studied fashion design at The Design & Arts College of New Zealand in Christchurch, I landed a highly prestigious job as creative and international relations manager for Wool Growers Marketing Limited, a national body of the New Zealand mid-micron wool industry. This newly-designed role required me to deeply engage with wool growers across remote, and vast farms in NZ, and setting them up for direct collaborations and partnerships throughout the world. Cutting through the role of traditional buying agents, I worked tirelessly to connect these growers to diverse brands and corporations across Europe, China, India, creating several successful innovative product lines. This work taught me the importance of staying focused on the core business while building an agile brand with global collaborators and riveting storytelling.

'I apply the same know-how, intuition and strategy to my eponymous fashion label back home in India. Season after season, we are focused on business first; yet we are always abuzz with collaborations with diverse brands and influencers alike. An authentic brand story—owning our Bengali legacy, and commitment to celebrating regional Indian weaves while reinterpreting them in a contemporary language and modern Indian aesthetic—empowers us to engage directly with editors and journalists for significant and meaningful press features.

'Having lived and travelled extensively overseas, I know first-hand of the burgeoning NRI population. When I started the Atelier, my vision was to create contemporary ethnic fashion for people living in India and across the world, this continues to be the retail mantra. Our tryst with e-commerce began four years ago with Aza Fashions, and we haven't looked back ever since. We retail online through most of the leading multi designer portals and continue to lead in our focus category of men's printed kurtas and chanderi sarees. Our off-line retail endeavours are equally strategic. We prefer to do multiple personalized trunk shows in our key markets around India and Asia at the right times in the year (before wedding season, festivities, etc). We also regularly schedule national roadshows at our partner retail stores in India, spread out over three to four days designated to influencer marketing and one-on-one appointments with our top clients.

'I started my Instagram handle during one of my trips to Europe, wanting to share vignettes from my adventures and inspirations I found at every corner. This has metamorphosed organically over the decade into a page that represents the culture, values and storytelling of the Pranay Baidya name and my wanderlust. Through the last couple of years especially, I am particularly dedicated to creating beautiful and meaningful campaigns with real people and influencers whose personal style we admire and find inspirational. Through cross channel re-posting, the campaigns reach both out to both our individual networks, fostering interest, engagement, inquiries and a considerable section eventually converting to retail business.

'As a creative enthusiast, I absolutely love ideating, planning, executing and content writing for our social media campaigns; almost equally to designing clothes! There is no alternative for determination, grit and a persuasive spirit. As a solopreneur one also needs a certain calmness and choosing and planning each move wisely. While I keep my eyes set on our long-term future vision, my energy and creativity are agile, weighing in new ideas and opportunities at every step. I have also discovered that intuition, coupled with strategy and brand story ownership is my best bet.'

How to Get Organized

Shakeel Sutarwala is my longest standing partner at Peepul, and he shared his essential advice on setting up a press office.

'A press office basically contains all the things you need to start reaching out to people and interact with the press—the brand bio, bios of your founder and other important people, visual assets such as photographs, videos, etc. It has everything that a PR campaign requires. When we work with a global brand, they give us dockets that have every kind of written and visual asset we might need, and that is the benchmark.

'The basics are the brand backgrounder and spokesperson bio, and some images whether those are of your product or of a campaign. A lot of this depends on the nature of the stories and the pitches planned. For instance, a brand may not have a product that can be photographed or a service to be promoted, but in that case, we're not going to need those images in any case to do our work.

'What is important to remember these days is that people don't have the time to read much, and they are bombarded from all sides, so what can do you to get attention? When I started out in PR sixteen or seventeen years ago, all the assets we shared were set in stone, but now the interesting challenge is that you can get very creative in how you build your press office and share that information. If a brand has two co-founders, for example, you could film them in conversation with one another, talking about the brand and what they stand for.

'A press office is not static and it never should be. You should keep updating it as the brand's journey progresses—a big launch or other milestone might need its own assets. As a matter of hygiene, it is a good idea to update founder images often, and find ways to freshen up the material as much as you can. Ideally, brands should be active participants in these and help their agency out.

'If you are working on your PR in-house, without an agency or publicist, setting up a press office will require you to work with a photographer, so please allocate a budget for that. Ideally, don't write your brand backgrounder and your own bio yourself. Find a way to engage with a writer or editor who can help you. It is always ideal to approach these with some degree of detachment so it would best to tell your story to someone, and have them translate that for you.

'When it comes to pitching to social and traditional media, the basics remain the same. You are sharing your story for them to amplify. What could be different are formats—it works better to be more direct and visual with social media, for example.'

GETTING STRATEGIC

The first thing to understand before you go about setting a strategy and systems in place is that publicity does not equate sales. What good PR does is create a mood board for customer sentiment and help you tell the stories that will eventually tie back into the business. For that to happen, what you need is consistent, effective storytelling and communication, which compounds over months and years in the minds of your customers and the media. Think about Chanel, for instance. Why do we covet everything the brand makes? (I cannot be alone in this, can I?) And why are we willing to sacrifice a luxury vacation for a bag or a jacket? On one hand, it's because that bag and jacket are just beautiful works of art. On the other, Chanel's storytelling, over decades, has created this desire in us to own a piece of it. The bottom line? Rome was not built in a day, so be patient and be persistent.

Now, as an agency, what we do when a potential client reaches out to us is a deep dive into their brand story and messaging. We want to know:

- What the vision for the brand is, in five years and then ten?
- What is the white space that they are going to occupy?
- What differentiates them from others in the market (we never want to associate with brands that are too derivative or work entirely off Pinterest references)?
- How interesting, imaginative, and promising they are?
- Their retail and business strategies.

If the founder and their team are willing to be honest and generous in the information they share, we are able to gauge quite quickly if this is a good fit for us or not. While the determining factors can vary between cases, I'd say that roughly what we are looking at are:

- The passion of the founder and the core team for their brand, because this shapes both the journey of the business and our relationship with them.
- The potential of the brand's idea: will it stand the test of time? Is there room for evolution and growth?
- The quality of their product/service: if we have to pitch it with conviction, we have to truly believe in it ourselves.
- What category the brand falls into and if we have the expertise and network to deliver on our promises to them.

LOOKING FOR A LONG-TERM PARTNER

Once a client signs up to work with us, we like to spend a month, give or take, to get to know them and draw up an effective strategic plan. At the end of this time, our goal is to create a messaging matrix, PR plan, and press materials and have a very clear roadmap of what we're going to focus on.

Before we start thinking about any of this, though, what is very critical is for us to understand and spend time on:

- Product positioning: where does it sit in the market?
- Overall positioning: does the brand want to be niche, a market leader or a thought leader?
- Business plan: what is the retail footprint?

If, for example, a brand wants to elevate its positioning, we focus on having the founder or core team members write op-ed pieces or other authored articles. Speaking opportunities and being part of panels is also a must-do. And if a new client wants to build its retail presence, we first start with building relationships with the business press. When it comes to products, we want to be very clear about what makes this particular brand unique—what is the white space it occupies? This then determines everything from shoots and product placements to features, reviews, influencer endorsement, and coverage of events or shows.

At the risk of sounding like a PSA, a publicist or agency can only do what they are empowered to do. We cannot come up with an annual plan (or) annual plans on our own. Clients who ask us to do this are usually the most collaborative. There are no magic hats in this business, and I know from experience that I can do the best work possible when the brand gives me all the information I need to become their expert champion. Especially in our current climate, a publicist is not just someone who gets the brand written about—we act as an advisory and strategic partner.

We don't look only at column inches of print coverage or number of posts on Instagram. At Peepul, our approach is very holistic, and we like to deep dive in order to build a narrative that will evolve over time. One of our core objectives is also to help our client educate their customer and engage with them in an authentic, sustainable manner and to find a community of brand champions, such as editors, tastemakers, influencers, and experts who will not just endorse a product but also help the brand in its own journey. A key point we like to emphasize with potential and new clients is to understand that PR does not affect your bottom line immediately. It helps build your brand and create an aura which eventually translates into business, and this is where being patient helps. Lastly, on a more practical note, all of this is what we also base our monthly, quarterly, and annual deliverables on.

What helps my team and me immensely is when clients are meticulous with their overall scope of work, budgets, product plan, marketing spends and calendars and if they are generous and collaborative in discussing these with us or having us be a part of some of these decisions, if and when required. A PR plan could be as long-term or short-term as the client wants, based on how organised they are. We love it when we get a calendar of events, launches, business milestones, and marketing activities, because it really helps us get creative and strategic with our PR calendar. For instance, if we know you are launching a new product in June, we can identify the right editors and influencers to chat with months in advance, so there is no danger of letting any opportunity slip past us.

There are two key points I like to consider for a client. One is a strategic timeline of twelve months, with four key moments and, ideally, an annual property that truly showcases its values and becomes its signature. And the second is a product that people immediately associate it with. With Kama, for instance, our aim was to create instant recall for its exquisite rose water. We also worked with them on a campaign called Cleanse Heal Rejuvenate, which served as an umbrella for events, online initiatives and press activity.

When we launched Kiehl's in India, we knew going in that they have an existing set of products and, unlike other brands, they do not have new launches very often. So we had to get very deliberate with our approach and decided to host an event in the monsoon to educate customers on how to take care of their skin using key Kiehl's products. In both these instances, our aim was to elevate a brand while working with what they had. You don't always need something new and exciting to create buzz.

Around the World

As we start working with brands towards international visibility, it's been interesting to watch businesses navigate a new dynamic. I reached out to James LaForce, founder and CEO of LaForce, a New York-based marketing communications agency that works with big-ticket names across the world. James has over thirty years of experience in media and communications, and is someone I look up to.

Could you talk a little bit about how the PR business has evolved in the last ten to fifteen years? Especially with the growth of social media, and influencer culture, how has brand communication changed?

While so much has changed, and change keeps coming, I try to stay focused on the elements of brand communications that endures: Personal stories are more compelling than business plans. We try to keep the focus on the people in the business, their unique contribution to the brand's success, how their personal histories inform the business, the products and the culture of their organization.

When a brand approaches you to represent them, what sparks interest for you?

Again, the people behind the brand are more important than the brand itself. If we believe a company has integrity, if the individuals in the company are realistic and demonstrate that they will listen to our counsel, accept our feedback and truly work together in partnership, then we are much more interested in exploring a working relationship. Secondly, their company and products need to have a reason for being, they need to be filling a void in the marketplace, offering products or services that are unique and offer a true consumer benefit. And now, more than ever, we strive to work with individuals and companies who demonstrate a commitment to preserving the environment, creating a positive social impact, and following the highest standards of corporate governance.

As we hear of Indian brands looking at going international, how can they get a respected agency's attention?

Americans are fascinated by all things Indian: food, fashion and travel. However, many of us have so much to learn about Indian history, culture and traditions. I think any Indian brand exploring growth into the American market, has to take on some aspect of educating those consumers about India's rich traditions. At the same time, the company needs to demonstrate its commitment to responsible manufacturing as it relates to women, children and the environment.

From your vantage point as a leading publicist, are there secrets to brand growth and longevity? What do the best brands get right, and what are the most common mistakes you see?

While every business and brand has to find its own unique path to success and longevity, there are the basic principles of transparency, humanity, equity and inclusion that no organization can succeed without. I think the most common mistake brands make is thinking that all growth is good. Growth is essential, but finding the right pace and direction for that growth can make the difference between longevity and failure.

Traditional media is changing at the speed of light but social media is still a fickle landscape. What's the balance you suggest to brands?

We will always prioritize earned coverage from credible media outlets over influencer content. Yes, we are thrilled when influencers choose to promote our client brands, and we do create strategies in which we compensate them for content around our brands. However, we don't let these efforts distract us from cultivating relationships with and respect from respected journalists. As more and more paid social content is perpetuated, it only makes the authentic, credible news coverage that much more valuable.

Do you see a change in what clients ask of you today as opposed to 2020? Where do you see this shift heading towards?

Even since 2020, there has been a growing interest for something our clients are calling 'corp-sumer' coverage. By that, they mean a story that blends the corporate narrative with the consumer benefits of the company and its products. For example, a story that describes how a new product is popular with consumers while also fulfilling the company's promise to create more environmentally-friendly products.

Taking Stock

All of the strategy, activity and coverage are only as good as the results they yield. What makes this tricky is that a lot of the impact of PR can be intangible, and, often, the pay-off comes much later. That said, knowing how to measure the outcome of what you do is essential. Sanjay Nigam is a consulting strategist and insights innovator at Perfect Relations, and I spoke with him about how he approaches this rather tricky subject.

You work at Perfect Relations, which I believe is the firm setting benchmarks in thought leadership and best practices in the Indian PR industry. Could you speak a little bit about how you approach measuring outcomes of PR activities?

Just to put this in perspective, Perfect Relations has been around for thirty years, and I have been with the agency for five. Before this my experience has been in news TV for more than twenty-five years. In both, results and outcomes sought by the media and PR are the same. When I worked in television, we measured outcomes by the TRPs. Every Friday, the editorial team assembled in a room, analyzed the TRPs, and if we did not reach our goal, we would look at what we were doing wrong.

Outcome drives PR just as it does TV. We are constantly asking ourselves – what are the results of our efforts, our choice of media, and the stories we have put out? Also connected is building a client's profile or creating brand recall. Either way, the outcome depends on the audience. So the first question is—who are you reaching out to? A client could come to us and say, 'I want this message to reach a particular stakeholder'—say the government. Another might say, 'I want the people running e-commerce sites to read about me, so we can work together.' A third may say, 'I am not concerned with 100,000 viewers. My audience is ten people in a certain government department.' And who that audience is determines the kind of media you choose.

Would you agree that the first thing to do is to set goals with a client? That helps both agency and brand align on the benchmark of measurement.

Earlier, you closed on a contract, drew up a plan and then followed it. PR has become fluid and all of us have to be agile. We have to turn on a dime because the media environment is changing at high speed. We are now looking at situations where we constantly need new strategies because every day has a new buzzword or trending topic. You have to contextualize your messaging in whatever is the meme of the day—this has become very important.

What matters to the PR agency is not just the perceptions of an audience but also that of the client. Open-ended discussions are vital, and your job is not just to meet pre-defined targets. Working with clients as a publicist now also means talking them through various situations, including crises, and being there for them all the time.

According to you, what are the useful tools to measure results and which are not?

If I had to speak in terms of advertising, PR value is the cost of an ad multiplied by five. But how do you measure editorial content and assign it a higher value? Do you add more points for awareness, recall, and credibility? Clients certainly expect quantity—the number of clips – but they also expect impact. What they want to know is – what was the information shared, how much of it was positive, and was there anything negative written or said about the brand that could create a problem?

Companies need peer analysis to give them a sense of how their messaging measures against the competition's. They ask: are we number one on the stack of newspapers and magazines this month? Who are the journalists writing about us, and are they A-listers? Did they give me editorial space that captures mindshare? Am I ahead of my rival by the number of positive impressions on social media? Will all of this coverage create an attitudinal shift in how people perceive my brand?

Engagement is what matters now with digital and social media. For instance, if a company launches a new product, they will do press events, send releases and work on building coverage. They will also look at digital and social media platforms to see how all of these were shared and the conversations that were triggered by them.

At the end of the day, it comes down to four things – positioning, quantity, quality and engagement.

How do you see the balance between social and traditional media?

I like to divide the pie into owned media (your website, blogs, etc), social media and traditional media (earned media). Traditional media is not dead just as yet (especially in India), and it will not be for a while. So you do have to build relationships with editors, journalists and other opinion makers; maybe even host press trips with no strings attached. It is a slow game and it takes time to get used to. A good PR agency or publicist always helps.

In India, social media is not strong enough just yet for you to ignore everyone else. While influencers are now a part of the landscape, often they are seen as interlopers, whose opinions are suspect because everything they say about a brand is paid for.

I sometimes have conversations with clients who value quality over quantity, and the reason I bring this up is

that it goes back to goal-setting. People see impact every differently. How do you work with clients who may want to stay discreet?

Most of the time, we are pushing clients to engage more with the media. If they are not confident, and if they need clarity, about what to say or how to say it, we take them through a structured media training designed for their needs.

There is no substitute for communication, whether the media reaches out to you organically or via your publicist. It does not help to stay out of the media. When you go to earned media, journalists will look at your digital and social media footprint—they want to know who you are and how much newsworthy heft you have. Studies have shown that business performance is one metric, but valuation rides on market sentiment—investors look at how people are talking about you.

So you have to talk, you have to communicate and your C-suite executives need to engage with the media to be perceived as credible. This is especially true in a crisis. If you take control of the narrative, it boosts your credibility and the brand's reputation.

Finally, what tips would you share with an entrepreneur who may not be able to engage with a publicist. How should they build out their brand communication and PR?

Entrepreneurs are driven by outcomes; they are strategic and conservative in their approach as they need to reach out to multiple stakeholders and yet must conserve cash. Start with building a great website. Invest in creating video and audio content to share on your social media platforms. Next, build a robust social media presence that helps you find your audience and engage with them. Be prompt and agile in your messaging and participate in conversations. It is easy these days to track engagement and study analytics, so do that often and calibrate your efforts.

Once you have critical mass in social media, hire a small agency or freelancer. Or you could sign up with a larger agency on a project. These options will help you build a plan to start formally engaging with traditional media. So, all of your messaging groundwork will add-up in the end.

CHAPTER EIGHT

Building Relationships and Getting Pitch Perfect

The one thing that has not changed about PR, no matter which country I am in or which industry I work with, is that this is the business of making connections and building relationships. My team has tired of hearing me say it and you might too, but I cannot emphasize this enough. When I was a young publicist, I sent faxes, and now the junior members of my team are on DM with people, which I would never dream of doing, but there you are. We have to keep adapting basic skills of relationship-building to modern mediums. And my purpose with this chapter is two-fold—as publicists, our cachet depends greatly on the networks we've built, and as a brand, you need to find and grow an audience, whether or not they are paying customers. So, the first matter at hand is to map a strong set of stakeholders.

What does it mean to build allies? That you create a community of people who believe in you, your brand and your product or service, and they will support you as you grow. You can think of a core group as your champions, who become a true part of the journey, and you might even rely on some of them for advice or opinion. And eventually, you want this connection to amplify your message to your consumer.

From a PR perspective, we used to secure editorials in premium publications because we wanted a writer or an editor's endorsement, which was far more valuable than any ad. Now, we look to influencers, who can sway the opinion of a consumer. But I have to caution you that it never works to think only about what you or your brand can get from a person, whether that is the editor of a magazine or an influencer with millions of followers on Instagram. One of my greatest lessons has been to always consider what the mutual benefit is. An ideal network is one built on generosity and authenticity.

In the pre-social media era, we would strategically list the journalists, columnists, and editors who would understand a brand or product because it is not only about a beat or publication, it is also about the person's interests.

Priya Tanna, the founding editor of *Vogue India*, has this bit of advice when it comes to creating healthy relationships with the media: 'It's not speed-dating, you're looking for a long-term partnership here. So, like any good relationship you need to nurture, communicate, invest, and trust. So, begin with first figuring out which media is right for their messaging. Once you have your shortlist, invest in engaging with them regularly and communicating clearly (and this is where a good PR strategy comes in) on who your brand is and what it does. A relationship also needs two-way traffic, so trust our expertise, get over story pitches and tell us your brand's story, and we'll find the right medium and format in which to translate that.'

Building Bridges

When I first met Nonita Kalra in the mid 2000s, she was the editor-in-chief of *Elle India*, one of the first international lifestyle magazines that had entered the Indian market. We had a friend in common, France Grand, but that knowledge did not make me feel any less intimidated by her. Nonita is an old-school editor who has built publications (she also headed up *Harper's Bazaar India*), shaped the business of storytelling and mentored brands. Now, she is editor-in-chief at Tata Cliq Luxury. I am less intimidated by Nonita these days, but my admiration for her ability to build meaningful relationships and tell deep stories remains the same.

'Relationships matter to brand-building. Earlier, a founder or entrepreneur, who created a brand and the media, which was the storyteller, built a relationship of equals. Both had a common view of the world, and it was about more than just fashion, beauty or politics. So in that traditional sense, these relationships were critical, and still remain so, even though the world is changing every day.

'In India, when the first fashion weeks started, a magazine helped the customer understand what a trend is, how to shop it, curate a wardrobe and keep updating their look. It could be compared to a sales job because we were creating a common language that customers, journalists, and designers could speak. There was an intellectual curiosity and you were working with equals.

'Right now, we are all in flux. All relationships are changing but we've seen this happen over and over. The death of print has been predicted many times and though we may need to learn a new language to communicate in, relationships will stay sacred even in that new world. My instinct says because everyone is flocking to social media and everyone is just looking at Instagram, it's dead. Every brand has to find what makes sense for it in the long term. For example, legacy brands must do coffee-table books because your story demands it and it will affirm why your customer wants to own your products forever. Just as the media is going through a churn, PR, too, is having to keep up with the new world. The PR industry in India limited itself by thinking only of column inches and Instagram (or social media) mentions. A few companies were sensible and started looking at working with clients on strategy and brand building – it is these agencies that have survived.

'I think that journalists and publicists need to work on rebuilding a community that has heft. We took the power out of our own hands by thinking small and a digital community has taken over. In India, influencers still support brands and the media and now is the time for everyone to co-create using strategic partnerships. We have to figure out how to monetise for each other so free PR and press can continue to exist. This is vital for everyone.

'As a consumer and as a player in the fashion and beauty industry, when I get to know the founder of a brand first, that's a bonus. Sometimes I may not know them, but their beliefs shine through in their brand communication, which is great. This brings me to memorable brands. The easy answer to creating a brand with longevity is innovation. Think out of the box, and focus on thought leadership. Create extensions that are relevant to your brand, and to a wide audience.

'My advice to brands has always been about the basics – think about who you are, who your audience is and what is the story that you are telling. You have to be authentic and I know this is an overused word but if you don't know who you are, how and what will you communicate? I encourage brands to stop hiding behind others and get over their hesitancy. Not everyone can run a marathon or do a headstand. So do what is right to you, and reach out to people who feel like a good fit. If you are a home-grown brand, you have the luxury to build your community with thoughtfulness and that's why it will last. I am very interested in young brands like Kulfi Beauty that tell the south Asian story. Or a brand like Pahadi Local that has always been focused in its communication and engaged with its customer.

'What I have always told the writers in my team also applies to brands when it comes to voice and storytelling - write like you speak, read your copy out aloud and enjoy what you stand for. Don't be in a hurry. Go from moment to moment, figuring out who you are. In fact, be worried if you grow too fast. Ask yourself often why you started the brand - is it your career, or your life's work? Slow down and do the work every day. You will find your unique place in the world. Don't be different just for the sake of being different. (What is unique to you might just be clichéd to others, but that's okay.) Be collaborative. No one survives on their own and building a universe of support will only serve you in the long run. There is no formula to storytelling so do what comes naturally to you. And tell your story again and again. If you don't get bored of it, why will anyone else?'

A WIDER CIRCLE

Now, where do you start when you want to build allies? First, go back to your notes on your target audience and understand who and what will they pay attention to. This will determine whether you put emphasis on traditional media or social media, though you will always need to reassess and readjust, in my experience. These days, opinions are shaped as much by celebrities, macro-influencers, and micro-influencers.

The most important thing is to feel the pulse of the market, in order to always know who are the people you must pay attention to. For example, in the past decade, fashion stylists have taken on a bigger role because they dress celebrities, and they can help a brand reach its target audience, either with their client lists or on their own merit. You want Kareena Kapoor or Virat Kolhi to wear your label? Their stylists are the key.

I am going to address the elephant in the room first—the celebrity factor. In India, if you collaborate with a film star, a television celebrity, or any other famous person, it immediately does wonders for your brand's messaging. That said, should you invest in these collaborations or hire an actress or other big-ticket name to be a brand ambassador? Not always. If you are in a niche market, going to multiple micro-influencers might actually work better for you. And if you do have all the data and the financial resources to go the movie star route, please choose wisely based on your own brand values and those of your customer. In my experience, clients who have brought on a big name have seen sales boosted. Their brand name gets recognized instantly by people they might never have reached under other circumstances. But it only has long-term value if their ambassador or collaborator is completely aligned with their brand.

The obvious instance of when your allies matter the most is a launch, whether of the brand itself, a campaign, or a new product or vertical. If it is a line of clothing or a collection of jewellery, we visualize who would be drawn to it, from editors and stylists to clients. For us, the first thing to consider is the concept and the mood the brand wants to set. To me, when you are conceptualizing a campaign or product, think of at least ten people it should resonate with, and you have enough of a sample group to work with.

Another important consideration now is online amplification, via authentic voices. A misfit match can make people cringe. We are very deliberate about the collaborations our clients create with influencers across the board. Do we need a hundred people to pass the message on, or will five do? Say I was putting together a new launch for a luxury brand, my preference would be to have three or four coveted names as opposed to a hundred people creating Reels with the same bag. We all know when an international brand has been on a gifting drive with a specific product. That's all I want to say. And the customer is not a fool. I often feel like people who choose volume can end up with a bit of an overload, and that is not a good thing.

We advise our clients to look at three benchmarks to measure success:

- Social media insights
- Leads and conversions, which showcase brand loyalty
- Sales

Building Trust in the Age of Influence

Ashutosh Munshi is the executive vice president and head of brand practice, Asia Pacific at Edelman India, a leading agency. I could think of no one better to talk about how influencers are changing the game, and what brands must do in order to keep up.

'Back in 2010, blogger was the buzz word for influence. Today, influencer marketing has entered a new era. It has become the career choice for Gen-Z, a side hustle for many and a marketing engine for brands that are looking to expand their reach and awareness, and drive conversions. What brands are missing out on is leveraging authentic voices to earn the right attention and build trust that drives growth.

The influencer marketing Industry in India is estimated at a whopping $75-150 million a year, according to AdLift. Influencers' consistency in delivering good-quality, relatable, and diverse content has earned them high levels of trust from their audiences, with the power to positively impact all stages of the path to purchase. A single post by a trusted influencer can lead to a product being sold out in a matter of minutes, but it can also devalue a company's worth by billions. Remember Kylie Jenner's tweet that cost Snapchat $ 1.3 billion? Like it or not, we are influenced by these voices in our every day choices, consciously or otherwise.

The many faces of influence

The role of the influencer has gone beyond the realm of social media content creator. They are now actors, fashion editors, red carpet representatives, brand campaign stars, co-creators of products, catalysts for social change, and more. In India, we saw influencers Kusha Kapila and Masoom Minawala walk the red carpet at Cannes, 2019.

There are very compelling reasons why influencer marketing is so critical. Some stats will provide a better perspective. These are sourced from an Influencer Marketing Outlook report by Buzzoka:

- 38 per cent of brand custodians feel influencer marketing is becoming more important with each passing year due to better reach and engagement

- According to 72 per cent of marketers, influencer marketing is the fastest growing online customer acquisition method

- 76 per cent of brands are looking to increase their budget this year compared to 62 per cent last year

But then, influence is not restricted to just celebrities and social media stars. Journalists and bloggers are also influencers in the earned-media space. And brands need to treat them as they do the stars. After all, credibility comes from unpaid third-party endorsement. Equally so, subject matter experts – doctors, academia, marketing experts, artists, chefs, professors and others – are also influencers. Brands must remain cautious of their influencer mix, as they build out campaign plans.

As the climate of social media is shifting, influencer marketing is becoming a more powerful force than ever by innovating constantly to firm its position and foster growth.

Influencer commerce, influencer incubation, virtual influencers, influencer community, social search optimisation, and creator-first studios are some of the Influencer Marketing trends that are on the rise, across the globe and in India. These trends have been adopted by evolved brands who have moved ahead in the influencer ecosystem and are now looking at influencers beyond the lens of awareness propellers.

Influencer marketing is gaining popularity across the country by virtue of regional influencers prevalent across platforms. We currently have 234 million Indian language users online, compared to 175 million English users. According to research, 7 in 10 people relate to influencers more than celebrities, and this is further improved if consumers read or watch content in a language that they understand, it connects with them and motivates them to take action. (These insights are from a piece by Ankit Agarwal published in Social Samosa, about the success of regional content and influencers.)

How authentic are these voices?

While there are several advantages dovetailed with influencer marketing, the one question that has plagued the industry for a while is this: how authentic are these voices?

Following the US and Brazil, India has the third highest number of bought followers in the world. From bots to fake followers to doctored engagement in the form of comments, fraudulent actors are working hard to stay one step ahead of platform algorithms, and brand reputation is at stake.

When it comes to bots, low-quality followers can be bought at Rs 2,500 for 10,000 followers; the same number of mid-quality and high-quality followers come at the price of Rs 3,500 and Rs 4,500 respectively.

It's no longer true that only a mega influencer with a large fan following will secure brand promotions; even micro influencers today can secure paid or barter brand promotions on account of their following.

In the words of Keith Weed, former global chief marketing and communications officer, Unilever, "The key to improving the situation is three-fold: cleaning up the influencer ecosystem by removing misleading engagement; making brands and influencers more aware of the use of dishonest practices; and improving transparency from social platforms to help brands measure impact."

Apart from vanity metrics, brands and their partner agencies need to look at psychological and contextual layers to form a more accurate portrait of influencers and their followers. For fraudulent activity, one can rely on online tools to sniff out counterfeit or fraudulent accounts and influencers who profit from them.

Keeping this in mind and with influencer marketing becoming mainstream in India, the Advertising Standard Council of India (ASCI) launched the Influencer Marketing Guidelines, making it mandatory for influencers to label all kinds of branded content to balance the interests of consumers, influencers, agencies, advertisers, and all other stakeholders.

ASCI pointed out that consumers have a right to know what content has been paid for by brands and the guidelines intend to bring in transparency and accountability to influencer marketing. These guidelines, which have been shared widely online, will spur more honest communication within the realm of brand marketing and impact brands in several different ways.

They will, hopefully, engender responsible communications, making creators and brands equally accountable for all types of influencer-led content in the digital ecosystem. These regulations could not have come sooner, given the exponential growth and mainstream stature that influencer marketing has attained so rapidly in India.

Built on the foundation of trust, the ASCI guidelines reiterate our longstanding commitment to authenticity and credibility. As per our Edelman Brand Trust Report 2021, there is a bigger need for trust today than ever before. This trust in brands cannot be bought, it has to be earned with action— by creating experiences with products/services or through earned media or peer conversation and other trusted channels. Influence, too, is far higher when trust levels are high. It is built when influencers have a personal connection or expertise related to a topic or issue and when they promote brands with utmost transparency.

Riding on the back of this reality is Edelman's influencer marketing offer called Trusted Influence. We create campaigns for brands using insight driven, earned-centric creative thinking, amplified through credible influencers that deliver true impact and return on investment. For a business to flourish, it needs to reach its consumers in a way that inspires trust, and influencers are instrumental in building it because people are more likely to believe the words of laypersons who speak from their personal experience rather than an advertisement.

ASCI's issue of the recent guidelines marks the foray of influencer marketing into mainstream advertising, depicting how influencer marketing has evolved. This opens a wealth of growth opportunities for influencers, influencer marketing platforms, agencies as well as brands looking to benefit from the fast-growing industry.

With influencer marketing at the cusp of transformation and on track to become a $15 billion dollar industry by 2022, brands and corporations must prioritise authenticity and trust as they look to leverage the popularity and success of influencer as a part of the marketing mix.'

Play the Game and Have Fun

Rasna Bhasin is a content curator and creator who works with leading lifestyle, fashion and beauty brands. She has taught me a lot about navigating social media, building content and leveraging influence for a brand, which is what she talks about here, as well. I admire Rasna's spirit and enthusiasm and the fact that she uses her platform for good, too. She is one of the few people who has the courage to take a stand and that sets her apart, in my book.

How would you define what you do?

Today it's a bit complex to pin point what I actually do. If I could simplify, I would say I am a curator, and a bit of a creator as well. I curate and create experiences and content for brands as well as the audience that follows me. I also assist brands in putting across their vision, help them strategise their digital presence, and work with them in marketing specifically online.

What do you see as the commandments for brands to do well with their social media?

The core values and beliefs of a brand need to translate online. Its honesty and essence needs to be felt across platforms.

Brands need to stay true to their identity and be able to connect to their audiences through a screen as well as they do at a brick and mortar store.

How do you see social media influencing branding and business? For example, how do you encourage your clients to measure these markers as they work with you?

It obviously started with the likes and followers but today I tell brands to measure it by relatability and recognition. A brand that is able to create a strong social media or digital presence has a higher recall value than other. Especially today where the world is physically disconnected and the only way to connect is online. So imagine everybody recognises a brand easily because they've been familiarised with it over a period of time digitally.

I strongly feel that the brand's offline and online communication should always be in sync. Online content might be able to influence a customer to walk into a space or store just because of the impact it created at a subconscious level in the consumer's mind. Any online association can and should be leveraged offline.

What do you see brands getting wrong when they collaborate with people or with one another?

A lot of times, brands tend to calculate everything in numbers. While numbers are extremely important, so are relatability and relationships. Collaborating with a person who doesn't believe in the same values as the brand, or vice versa just because of their high number of followers doesn't work most times. I find it easier to relate to micro-influencers or celebrities than macro ones.

A celebrity endorsement is great to make a brand famous, so to speak but a smaller influencer who is more relatable to the audience might be able to convince the consumer to buy the product or try a service. So while celebrities work well in getting people to become aware of the brand, smaller relatable personalities help in converting them into consumers.

What makes social media fun to work with? If you had to predict where Instagram is headed for brands, what would you say?

It connects you to anybody you want to be connected to. You could be sitting in one corner of the world and discovering something on the other. It brings everyone together and makes the world smaller. It makes things accessible, helps you learn and discover.

Because of social media, you become extremely well-informed about what you're planning to buy and the options you can choose from—there's something for every sort of consumer.

It's fun to work with social media because you can create what you visualise and get as wild as you want to, read real-time feedback and explore the world with one click. Instagram is here to stay. I think we can utilise it to the best of our abilities. It's also not just limited to brands and sales, so think bigger.

How to Win Friends and Influence People: The 2.0 Edition

I chatted with Shakeel Sutarwala, Partner at Peepul and a publicist with decades of experience, to put together a primer on networking.

'Social media makes building a community seem easy but it's not. There's a voyeuristic aspect to just following people, but to have that translate into a relationship, you have to put in the work. And this is not a numbers game—your real network can be the five right people, not 500, as long as it translates for you.'

1. The first thing to do is to approach the whole exercise as one of cultivating relationships and not just networking,

which can sometimes feel like a transactional activity. Of course, some relationships are purely transactional and that's fine, but this should be the exception and not the rule.

2. Get out of your comfort zone, please. If you are a publicist, don't just hang around with other publicists.

3. No matter what your personality, you can find a way to do this. If you are anxious, train yourself to be comfortable in social situations by taking baby steps. Maybe have a series of one-to-one conversations at a party rather than hanging out in a group? Or plan your entry and exit, and spend the time wisely on chatting with the right people.

4. Phone a friend! Ask them to come with you to an event or introduce you to people they think you should know. And vice versa.

5. Be interested and interesting. No one wants to listen to your stories for an hour or be interviewed endlessly. You have to strike a balance.

6. I always like to see people for a coffee or a drink. It's much more relaxed than a meal, and you can chat about work or life for an hour or two.

7. Have a pool of stories to break the ice with someone, whether you're seeing them for a glass of wine or at a crowded party. Don't worry about repeating yourself.

8. Always research the person or people you are going to meet, so you can find commonality.

9. Get good at small talk. The weather, restaurants, and traffic, for instance, are topics everyone has a lot to say about. I don't understand people who believe they cannot master small talk. It feels idiot-proof!
10. Be self-deprecating. No one enjoys chatting with someone who takes themselves too seriously.

Do It Right, Every Time

Noor Enayat, is one of my partners at Peepul, and has a reputation for being a straight talker. Which is why I asked her for her thoughts on how publicists can build meaningful, productive relationships with the media and their clients. Because both matter very much.

'The golden rule to remember is that the time of the journalist or media person you are interacting with is as precious as yours. Therefore, it is essential to gradually build a rapport for them to know that each time they speak to you, they will walk out of that conversation with something new or exciting that they can use at some point in the future.

Over the years, my relationship with a lot of journalists I often work with has become personally professional. What this means is that I am not only in touch with them for my clients but also on regular basis on every day things. I often try and help them with contacts, information on stories entirely unrelated to my business, making our equation non-transactional.

It is also crucial that we as colleagues in the same larger industry take time out to check on each other every day without being intrusive. You both work in the same larger ecosystem. Therefore, it is essential for them to see you as an individual and not only as a representative of a brand or an agency. So, what one does is what you would do with a colleague in the office, i.e. send a message from time to time asking them if all is well. Or if you hear about something that is happening in their life, offer help or be there to talk about it, if they would like to.

Also, in non-peak season, I keep my brands relevant to these people by actually talking to them about the people behind the brand. So it is imperative to move the narrative to be one about the individuals behind the brand and not putting your client on a pedestal but speaking about them as everyday people you know.

One of the best examples I can give is of someone like Mrs Anita Lal of Good Earth, who I deeply admire for the person she is and her work. My admiration for her does not come from the brand's products but from the process that she follows, her conviction in what she does, and overall empathy as a human being towards the people she works with.

Similarly, when I speak of another of my favourite clients— Tarun Tahiliani, I don't just talk about the clothes he makes; I talk about the person he is. And how that person reflects in his clothes—his deep understanding of craft comes from 25 years of curiosity and learning; the lightness in his garments comes from not looking at fashion from the lens of just grandeur but also ease; and his love for silhouettes and drapes comes from his study of the art of draping that dominates traditional Indian dressing historically. But I also talk about his phenomenal sense of humour, an ability to laugh at himself and his work, his passion for India in all its forms and his idea of the country, which is very similar to mine.

So, in essence, one has to develop human relationships with people. These can't be transactional only, you must work at keeping them mutually beneficial in terms of conversation, insight, and empathy.'

Cross Your Ts, and Dot Your Is

Manju Sara Rajan, editor, *Beautiful Homes*, is a quiet force in the design and art world. She previously headed *Architectural Digest India* and was the CEO of the Kochi Biennale Foundation. Manju has had a long and varied journalistic career, and I respect her confidence and editorial eye. Which is why I requested her to write about what makes a pitch compelling.

'It was the best of times, but we didn't know it then. We didn't know that we were working through print media's last decade of infallibility. That digital media—long considered the sidekick of the glossies, which was always left to trail the afterglow of print – would stage a takeover; an elimination even. Those changes also wrought turbulence on the ancillary activities that are part of the media world. Like public relations. For so long, the paradigm hadn't changed and now almost nothing remains the same. Mastheads are constantly transmogrifying as media titles deal with financial chaos, lead times are more urgent, and editorial stories are lobbed together under the numb term "content". Who really needs a magazine when everyone is telling stories? And anyone can create content . . ..

I began my career as a news magazine reporter, then moved to newspapers, lifestyle magazines and art management. In the last few years, I've been in the digital media space as the editor-in-chief of Beautifulhomes.com, a platform for decor and design. My observations here are based on my understanding of the way stories are pitched and published in the world of print and digital publications. Some things have changed. Some things remain reassuringly same. Throughout this section, you've read the agency perspective, and I'd like to offer the side of the editor.

1. **What is a pitch?** Simply put, it is a story angle. Journalists can be lazy (though we'd never admit it) but when you get an idea from an agency, sometimes it does the trick. Thinking about an angle, a perspective that suits both the brand you represent and befits the title you're presenting it to is a win-win.

2. **How does one create a pitch?** Do the homework. Understand the masthead, the nuance of coverage, and who you're pitching to. Invest in learning about the publication, its people. Look at the bylines and the voice of the publication, so the pitch is effective and useful for both sides. Another really important detail—spellings and grammar. Taking the time to look at the spellings of people's names. Run a check on grammar. This is really, really important. Everyone is judgemental of everyone but themselves, and it is worth remembering that an agency represents the brands they work with, so invest in copy-editing.

3. **Who are you talking to?** With high-value proposition stories like an exclusive interview or long feature, it is important to think about the person who might cover the story and offer the piece while keeping in mind the interest and tone of the writer.

4. **Build mutual respect.** I'm very wary of agencies and PR representatives who treat their clients like they're human Fabergé eggs and journalists like scuttling meerkats. When accosted by PR representatives who control access to clients as though writers may turn into competition, my reaction is to say, "Well, keep them."

I understand there are pitfalls to direct communication between a media publication and a client but that is why a nuanced approach is important. Understand who you're dealing with and guide your client accordingly. Your client ought to be your partner in the effort so you should both have an understanding of the media brand and team you unitedly speak with, and how it can be mutually useful. To control access to the point where a client has received coverage but no relationship has been built with the media title is a wasted opportunity.

5. **Again, focus on relationships.** Public relations—the name says it all. Creating a relationship with a media brand and its team is crucial for an agency and for their clients. Sometimes nurturing relationships means creating opportunities for people even if there isn't direct benefit in the short term.

One of the reasons Srimoyi has been able to forge long-term associations in the media is really because of that. I can think of a number of times where she's suggested ideas or made a connection even when there was nothing in it for her. But it creates a chain of good deeds that helps build a relationship, trust and mutual benefit eventually. On another note, it is worthwhile to remember that today's junior writer is tomorrow's editor. I'm not a fan of agencies that treat my team badly but pull out the red carpet for me. It's worthwhile to look at every name on an editorial team and create a blueprint for different levels of associations with each person on it.

6. **Where is your brand's audience?** What do they watch and listen to? It helps to navigate the spectrum of media you're dealing. Instead of chasing everyone, pitch different story angles to different media based on the audience each is speaking with. For positioning, print is still key. For reach, it's digital all the way. Traditional print magazines still treat digital as an add-on even though barely anyone buys magazines anymore. So choose your platform wisely, based on where your client's audience is listening and what stage of life the brand is at.

The popular trope of the relationship between PR and media is that journalists hate PR. But really one couldn't do its job fully without the other. For that relationship to work, requires a bit of time, a bit of brining, but it's worth the trouble.'

CHAPTER NINE

Save the Date

I have to confess that I love events. Whether it is a big-ticket launch, a perfectly executed trip, or an intimate dinner, it can create a deep engagement with the brand and leave you with a wonderful memory of an important interaction with not just the team but also other stakeholders. A good event can help you feel immersed and invested in the brand's universe. It offers an occasion for the community to get together and mark a moment. I know that COVID-19 has changed our reality, but everyone is going back to at least having a glass of wine together, and I feel like the essential elements of personal interaction will not change.

Apart from the intangible aspects of it, an event also raises awareness, much like a giant billboard would. Why do designers participate in fashion weeks? A show gets them publicity, a bank of images, and attention, apart from the chance to meet potential clients, buyers, editors, and other important people who can help them grow their business. They can get feedback directly and also share their creative process or point of view. And all this is along with the credibility you automatically get when you are part of an important event like a fashion week.

There are two ways of looking at events—one is a launch or similar landmark moment such as an anniversary, and the other is an annual or ritual property that a brand creates to gather their allies as they continue to expand their network. A good example of the latter are the Vogue Beauty Awards, India Today Seminar, Grazia Young Fashion Awards, AD Design Show, etc. These are events that the industry marks on their calendars and looks forward to because they gather the best in the business under one roof with a clear agenda.

I always attend events and encourage my team to do so because interactions and conversations are critical to the work we do. Especially in India, where there are no notable professional networking circuits or software with databases—both of which are crucial in cities like Paris or New York—an event is the only platform you have to talk about what you do and meet interesting people you need to know. Chatting with an editor at a store launch might help me learn what she has on her mind for her magazine's upcoming issues, and an influencer is more likely to share her vision and goals when we meet rather than over a perfunctory email exchange. This kind of information matters very much to publicists because we are our client's eyes and ears.

Fashion weeks and other industry events are particularly key, and my team and I show up even if we don't have clients participating. Just looking at the front rows at shows can give us a sense of what is happening in the business. Over the years, the MVPs have evolved from just editors, stylists, and buyers to bloggers and now film stars, celebrities, and influencers. That one row tells us who is driving conversations and shaping opinions.

One of my landmark experiences was working with the India Art Fair, which is such a large-scale event that brings together a whole industry and enthusiasts. It is both B2B and B2C, because galleries have viewings that are accessible to the public, but as a publicist, you also attend lunches, dinners, cocktails, and talks. Events of this magnitude have a life of their own, and what is essential is to make sure that you're constantly keeping track of not just the big picture but also all the myriad details that could make or break it.

Another important exercise from a brand-building and PR standpoint is a trip organized to a place that is of significance to a brand. For instance, Chanel flies editors to Paris to visit Coco Chanel's apartment or to its fields near Pégomas in France to see Mul roses being harvested to make the iconic perfume, Chanel No. 5. We always enjoyed taking a select group of people to Pondicherry for a visit to Hidesign's office and factory or to Bangalore and Kanjeevaram to understand the heritage and values of House of Angadi, a 600-year-old legacy brand that is now reinventing heritage weaves and fabrics for the modern market. These trips give editors and influencers a sense of the brand's roots. Once you introduce people to a brand's provenance, you make a connection that can only grow and evolve in the right direction.

CONCEPTUALIZING AN EVENT

I firmly believe that an experience has to help build storytelling inside the brand or get people to tell stories about you. Of course, you want to celebrate an anniversary, milestone, or announcement, but the most successful events capture the heart and DNA of a brand. In 2020, for instance, we had the chance to work with our client Tarun Tahiliani on a marquee event to commemorate the brand's twenty-fifth anniversary. Tarun is not just a very successful designer with a coveted label, he has also played a very important role in the growth of the Indian fashion industry. Whatever we planned for it needed to be memorable.

Working with TT (as everyone calls him affectionately) and his team, we chose twenty-five fashion champions who would fly into Delhi from across the country to spend a day with him, visiting his factory, listening to him talk about his work, and looking through his archives. It was an intimate and very rare opportunity for his community to understand Tarun's journey with his brand. This was followed by a fashion show at the Qutub Minar, and a party for 125 people at Tarun's home.

It is key to get your concept right. Spend time polishing the thought, based on your goal for the event, and your brand's personality. If you are a light-hearted brand, please do not host a sit-down dinner, unless it is themed after the Mad Tea Party. It also helps to think about what people expect from you and your brand and what might become a signature theme or detail that will add to your story over the years to come. Good Earth, for instance, puts on meticulously-planned launch events for their annual design collection, and you come away from each one with beautiful memories and quite awe-struck by the storytelling and execution.

Once you have your concept, draw up a thoughtful and diverse guest list. You always want to have the right mix of people: those who will create a buzz online and offline, your greatest supporters, partners, and collaborators, and of course the people who buy from you. Think about the conversations you want to foster and the dialogue you aim to create space for.

The people at the event make it memorable, so this is a very crucial to-do on your list. And as a publicist, it is the one I pay most attention to, whether it is my event or a client's. In some cases, it helps to have a few people co-host and curate a very unique guest list because the event merits diverse points of view or is so large-scale that you need extra hands to make sure you fill the room. Remember that a party can go very wrong if conversations sour or there are people there who clearly do not fit in.

We have all left a party in fifteen minutes, at some point, and that is the worst experience for everyone involved in organizing it.

While we're on the subject, the act of inviting is one that I wish people paid more attention to. The first invite must always go from the host and be as personal and warm as possible. Be witty if you have to, and use whatever technological wizardry you'd like to, but make sure you send an invite that people want to say yes to. Have someone in your team or your publicist's team follow up, and be accessible to guests who might have queries or requests. And a thank-you note afterwards adds a lovely touch which every guest appreciates.

With a concept and guest list in place, please devote time and attention to a lead-up and tease the event. This is especially important if you're planning a launch. When we worked with beauty retail giant Sephora on the launch of their store in Mumbai, we sent bespoke packages of make-up to a set of beauty bloggers, and they helped us create buzz around the launch before it happened. To close this loop, also think about what you can do after the event to keep conversations alive and make sure that all your hard work isn't gone in a few hours.

For a PR agency, the work starts as the event ends. Whether that's at 4 p.m. or 3 a.m., we immediately need to get the groundwork done to ensure coverage. Images have to be sent to the press and influencers, who can share them on their platforms and generate real time post-event buzz. We work with the brand to make sure their own social media platforms are updated with images, captions, stories, reels, and whatever else is #important at the time. Finally, we start thinking about how to capitalize on the coverage and attention that the event has brought us.

But, a word of caution. Not all events are easy to conceptualize or put together. I have personally had quite a few gnarly instances and as a company, we've navigated several tricky situations. Clients might not always be on the same page. Partners could end up being very difficult to deal with. Celebrities cancel or reschedule at the last minute. People can get offended because they were not asked or offended because they were not asked the right way.

I have come to believe that you have to be prepared for everything to go wrong but act like nothing will. If someone is unhappy and you hear of it, get on the phone and talk about it—a conversation inevitably smooths things over better than an email or text message can. Always have a plan B for every eventuality. And no matter how frustrating things get, do not lose your cool. It sounds clichéd, but this is vital—part of fronting a brand is learning how to take the rough with the smooth.

Ground Zero

Vandana Mohan, founder, The Wedding Design Company, is synonymous with events. From working on big-ticket corporate and luxury brand events to now executing iconic weddings, she is one of the best in the business. An old friend and someone I have worked with, I requested Vandana to talk about how to throw the perfect event.

'The role that events play in brand-building is one of affirmation. They tell the audience what the brand is all about. The experiential moment that an event creates for any brand is something that you cannot get off an ad. Whether it is virtual or in the real world, events give you a view and vision into what a brand is all about and what you could do with it.

'We all know what Chanel does, but until and unless I actually see, feel, and am transported into its world to see what the brand wants to show me, the connection is not so deep. Many of us don't have the imagination to do this on our own. And this is true for aspirational brands, too, not just luxury ones. Ultimately, I think events actually put life into a brand.

'What makes a brand event successful?

'One is definitely the audience. Here I am not talking about the influencers, editors, writers, or publicists. Yes, they're important, but not as important as the real people who are the ultimate brand users. An event needs a good mix of people, who feel comfortable in the space that they are in. Especially for a luxury brand, today, the consumer profile is changing. It's not only just the well-heeled who are invited, who are the buyers of a brand. It's the aspirational customer who wants to get there, too. So if a premium champagne brand is hosting a sit-down dinner, they have to be sure that they perhaps let go of a little formality to make all guests feel welcome.

'Great execution is very essential. It's the experience that one creates, as I said, to transport guests into a different world— one that the brand wants to showcase to their consumers. And, of course, great food, and a great bar. Experiential marketing plays a big role here, too. You want to show your clients how to use your product in every possible way. I might look at something and imagine one way to fit it into my life. A brand has to show me how to expand that lens.

'For me, in my job, it's very important to understand what the brand wants to say. I may have a perception of them, but when they approach me to do an event, I need to understand why they're doing it. What is the message that they want to share? They've got to be able to trust a vision that we create for them. We should try and be as close to that vision that we want to be. We shouldn't get lost in the fluff.

'I think I keep saying this again and again, but it's very important for the brand to identify their audiences and then cater to them. There are those people who know you and what you do. And those who don't, but you want them to come into your world. Brands are reaching out to every kind of person today, and experiential marketing is the one way where you actually get the consumer to try things. And that's why I think today, as we're seeing with Instagram and the digital world, everything is delivered to you in a package for you to experience, touch, feel. And maybe convert you into the consumer finally. So, yeah, I think it works wonderfully.'

GROWING A BUSINESS

As I mentioned earlier, I find that moving cities or countries is a way for me to reset my life and try something completely new. A change of scenery makes that journey that much easier and that much more real for me. Peepul was growing well in New York within the niche we had created for ourselves, catering to Indian brands (whether founded in the US or elsewhere) who wanted to speak to the Indian diaspora or find their way into the larger market. I know I've said this before, but it bears repeating in this context—my dream was always to move to India. Yes, New York was exciting and wonderful, but I was able to observe the Indian market on personal and work trips back and saw kernels that really appealed to me.

This was in the mid-2000s, and it was a time at which India was really changing. Fashion and lifestyle were on the cusp of growth and explosion, and I was very excited by the potential these industries had. I could take my learnings, hopes, and dreams from Paris and New York and translate them into reality in India. Which is what I set out to do when I finally made the move from New York to Mumbai, with my little dog Bali. I only had my sister and a few friends to fall back on. It was scary, but I had really prepared for this move, so all the anxiety was outweighed ultimately by my excitement to start this new chapter of my life.

In both Paris and New York, and every other large hub, a fashion publicist has an extremely clear-cut job. But in India in 2008, when I started dipping my toe into the pool, the industry was not as defined, so I had the very fortunate chance to make things up as I went along.

I was fiercely ambitious and hungry to make a mark. I had never worked in India aside from an early internship at the *Times of India* in Delhi when I was quite young, so I had to learn quite quickly to decode the work culture, understand industry practices, and read cues which could make my job of acquiring clients easier. What were clients missing? And were there aspects that they did not even know to miss? How could I become indispensable?

The first thing I started doing was scouting the market in two ways. One was to scope out the labels, brands, designers, entrepreneurs, movers and shakers who were building and shaping the fashion, beauty, and lifestyle markets. The second was to read every bit of press there was. This was the time that glossies were really picking up speed. *Elle India* and *Cosmopolitan India* had been around for a decade or more. *Vogue* had just launched. And there were homegrown brands such as *Verve*, *Beautiful People*, and *Indiawali Brides*. There was an electric buzz in the air. Readers and consumers were curious and willing to spend their money on whatever was new and exciting.

There was of course a public relations industry, packed with agencies that focused on luxury and fashion, but the dynamic of the business was very different. Clients ran the show, publicists followed briefs, and everyone measured success by column inches. I aimed to create a new way of working, in the Indian context. With the growth of the fashion press and a lively audience that was open to every possibility, what I wanted to do was take a deep dive with my clients, working with them on their brand, narrative, and publicity. I did not want to be handed a brief. I wanted to help them shape the brand's journey and be one of its gatekeepers. This was the white space I identified after a year or more of being in Mumbai.

Luckily, my New York contacts led me to create a very supportive ecosystem in India. A dear friend and fashion veteran Fern Mallis introduced me to Vikram Raizada, who was head of fashion at IMG at the time. He has, over the years, become a dear friend, and he helped me find my feet in the early part of my career in Mumbai. Some of my clients in the US were also happy to let me continue consulting with them from India, since they either had roots in the country or tangible associations, and this offered me financial stability that I did not take lightly. It also gave me new opportunities; for example, one client asked me to work on shoots for them and it helped me build a new skillset.

When I eventually started pitching actively for Indian clients, I wanted to offer them novelty—the fact that I could work with them in a 360-degree manner and that I brought my international experience to the table, which automatically encouraged them to also think big. Whether or not a brand or designer had dreams of world domination, I wanted to help them work through that lens. If they were part of Fashion Week, for instance, I offered to also be a part of the behind-the-scenes work, helping edit collections or style shows. (At the time, stylists were not the power players they are now, and designers relied on friendly fashion editors to help them out.) I essentially wanted to have a hand in creating the content and storylines, which I then pitched to the media.

Were clients ready for this? Not really. I had to work hard to convince them to give me a chance, and it did not always work out, but that's life and entrepreneurship. Payal Singhal, who had been my client in New York, also hired me in Mumbai, and she was a wonderful and patient guide who held my hand and counselled me. There were fundamental differences that I had to make my peace with. In India, being too commercial as a designer was considered a bad thing, and Payal helped me understand that. Payal would skillfully reinterpret reviews and saw her ability to marry commerce with creativity as an asset, and I learnt to see it in the right context. Payal was the best person to teach me this lesson because she always knew what she wanted, which was to please her customer, not a reviewer. This made her journey a bit unorthodox but she is now one of the stalwarts in the business.

I had another client who I agreed to work with even though I did not personally believe in her designs. When her show was panned roundly by reviewers, she blamed me for the bad press and I made the mistake of telling her that I, too, did not think her collection was as good as it could be. Of course, we had a bad falling out, and it taught me, perhaps, the most valuable lesson of my entrepreneurial life—never work with someone whose brand and offering you cannot get behind personally.

Since then, I have been brutally honest with myself before signing on a client—do I see myself defending them no matter what? As a publicist, you have to be able to market, promote, and support your clients' products and services unequivocally.

I also want to point out that at the time, the press in India was very exacting. They tried and tested products and services and would take the stand that they felt was the right one. You could not control that narrative and it was a bad idea to try, so it was also important for me to make sure clients understood that. A critique could be very helpful if a founder or designer was willing to listen and make appropriate changes.

A lot of hard work in the first year or two, with a suggest "skeleton team", more commonly used team, eventually allowed me to rent an office and suggest 'establish a real shop'. I never set up Peepul with the dream of building an empire or striking financial gold. Here, I just want to point out that the unique and wonderful thing about public relations is that the business works at any scale. You have worldwide networks such as Edelman, Burson-Marsteller, or MSL, to name a few. These are large global conglomerates who have large global corporations as clients. And then there are very high-end PR agencies that represent celebrities across industries, and this is a very specialized business. Medium-sized independent companies could have regional networks, either within a country or outside of it. Next up are boutique firms, like

Peepul, which are mid-sized and serve a niche audience. And finally, of course, there exists a lively network of freelancers or small shops run by two or three people.

I have always wanted Peepul to stay boutique in size and spirit. What I personally love and continue to be motivated by is the fact that we are in the business of relationships. Our business is high on emotion and personal rapport, and I was clear that my company should retain its soul and grow in an inclusive way, embracing the team, clients, and other stakeholders. What I had noticed is from my time in Paris and reinforced in New York as a client myself, was that people appreciate a PR agency that is high on EQ and offers a personal touch and excellent service. These have been my benchmarks for Peepul, apart from the fact that I want to manage relationships with my clients. At the end of the day, if the team and I can have a friendly, fun meal with our clients, that's the biggest win for me.

I never wanted to run a process-driven firm. On a more practical note, I chose agility over process because that's what made sense to me. Public relations, as a business, has a shelf life, and as the media and market landscapes change, so does PR. For a firm like Peepul, agility is priceless because we can always accompany the growth and brand requirements of our clients. When I started plotting our course while writing this book, I realized that we have always been in flux. In the first two years of being in India, Peepul had marquee clients such as Hidesign, Forevermark (a De Beers company) and Swarovski. I realized that I needed to build relationships with publicists or similar-sized agencies that had local networks in order to better service our clients, who trusted us enough to work in this manner. So outside of Mumbai and Delhi, we built a network of peers who could get our clients coverage in regional and vernacular press. Eventually, I did open offices and have dedicated teams in Delhi and Bangalore because these turned out to be hubs for most of our clients and it allowed us to consistently control the quality of work. But I also maintained relationships with most colleagues we partnered with.

There's something to be said about inclusivity in business, especially in an industry that has very little governance or regulated best practices. I still rely on a close network of colleagues for advice or industry intel.

Within ten years, Peepul grew from a team of two to a team of forty. The pandemic of COVID-19 unfortunately shifted these numbers for us, but as of this writing, we're still a good-sized team with presence in three cities. And the point is whether you work alone, with twenty people or as part of a large hundred-member team, you have to be able to build systems and a foundation that allow you to pivot whenever required. I always buy time by moving cities, which gives me the opportunity to reinvent. The kernel of an idea about this book came to me in Mumbai, I started writing it in Delhi and am now finishing it in Goa, where my family and I moved to at the beginning of 2021. I would not recommend this method to everyone, of course, but the point is that each of us, regardless of designation and industry, needs to reach within ourselves for tools of change and reinvention.

What has always helped me, apart from packing boxes and setting up homes, is being in conversation with people from other industries and reading a lot. It allows me to find solutions out of the box and apply inherited wisdom to my own reality.

3

GRIT:

Taking
risks &
getting
granular

CHAPTER TEN

Ring for Change

I am not sure if this is good or a bit neurotic, but every year since the inception of Peepul, I've always been thinking of how to reinvent what we do. In my mind, it is the only way for us to stay relevant because there are no constants in this business. Everything—the media, brands, and lifestyles—is in a constant state of flux.

You can look at change through the lens of scale, expansion, or scope of work. And in my experience, constant reinvention is as important as a classic pivot—it can lead you to the big idea much more organically. I can give you two solid examples here. The first is that as our client list in India began to grow, I wanted to have a showroom in the office where we displayed edited collections from the brands we represented. The purpose of the showroom was to build product placement and coverage for our clients, as stylists could source from us for shoots, events, or commercial engagements. It was an idea I was very committed to because any respectable lifestyle and luxury PR agency in Paris, New York, or Milan has one. It offered the perfect meeting point for PR, branding, and sales. Once we set it up, its success validated my faith in the project. Stylists stopped by very frequently and often ended up supporting a couple of our clients, which was a win-win for everyone. Initially, everyone on the team chipped in to help manage it, but we soon had a dedicated team of stylists to run it. This is also why I love working in India—for all the challenges, I have found such satisfaction in experimenting with quick reward and generous support.

The big pivot for us was taking the showroom online, which had been on my wish list for some years and was a big dream for me. As everything came to a standstill during the pandemic in 2020, we found the time to make it happen. Quite quickly, it has given us access to regional markets and a wider audience of celebrities and influencers. This matters very much because of the vastness of the country and the fact that it can be quite fragmented, plus the power of celebrity culture in India is huge. A movie star or cricketer wields influence like no one else can. This is a country that worships the cult of the high-powered individual. Creating space for that as an agency has been important for us and our clients.

The second example is of how we've approached social media as an agency. Starting a separate wing to offer social media content and management services would be the most practical and obvious option, but that's not a route I have wanted to go down, and neither does my team. What we have chosen to do is walk the path of an advisory. If a client needs help with social media, we first strategize for them and then bring on excellent partners who are experts in the field to work with them and us on building content. Reinvention could have been the answer here, but it did not sit right for any of us at Peepul, but we know that we cannot ignore the #elephantintheroom. This middle path has made a lot of sense for us and our clients and is proving to be a successful model, where we stick to our expertise but collaborate with others in order to stay competitive and relevant.

Not all ideas work, of course. I was once told a story in the context of restaurants—that you might open one which does phenomenally well, and that encourages you to open another. And then a third, but that one needs too much of your attention. So you lose focus on the first and the second, and before you know it, your business is in the red. I made a similar mistake in 2012–13.

When I moved to India, I kept some of my New York clients because that made for an easier transition and, let's be clear, the cash flow helped me immensely. And honestly, I was having a hard time cutting the cord with my New York chapter, which I had worked so hard to build along with my colleagues and partners there. It was taxing because I worked both Indian and New York business hours, and that left me with very little time for myself. In 2009, as the Indian business began to stand well on its own, I let go of the American end of things with much sadness and some relief at being able to have a life of my own. A couple of years later, I decided to reopen Peepul in New York because I had inquiries and felt like I wanted to give it another chance.

I rented an office and hired a young person to run it, while also travelling back and forth myself every couple of months. While we did get some leads and clients, it just turned out to be a bad decision for multiple reasons. Primarily, the person I hired was too young to handle the scope of work I had outlined for her, and I just did not have the time or energy to manage things with her. One could also say that I had not only thought through my decision. Secondly, the constant travel adversely affected my business in India, apart from being very expensive. After a point, I had to cut my losses, shut the NY operations down, and commit to focusing solely on India. The minute I did that, our work here began to grow by leaps and bounds.

This was not because of some mysterious forces, but because splitting time and resources was proving to be unprofitable on all sides. It was very upsetting for me, of course, because it felt like a failure. I had a made a series of wrong calls but, eventually, my own vision became clear to me. I must add here that I had not been thorough with a lot of my contractual documents, which led me to handle many liabilities. I hated (and still hate) handling the operational side of being an entrepreneur, but this was a big lesson learnt. You cannot hand over such foundational matters in a company without keeping a hawk's eye on all aspects. I trusted people around me because I didn't care to get involved. I signed documents without getting legal advice and relied on friendly recommendations. I no longer do any of these. Word to the wise—if you run a small business, even if you have a trusted accountant, you need to understand the basics and read through contracts you sign with vendors or partners.

As an optimist, I always try to focus on what something teaches me, and the valuable lesson here was that power and/or growth do not always come from scale. And that the traditional definition of expansion is not for everyone. My upper limit is forty people, and having the ability to be closely involved with the team and our clients is important for me because of the nature of the work we do. Also, being restless doesn't always help and is in no way a good symptom for ambition.

PIVOTING IS PIVOTAL

Public relations is a business that is constantly pivoting. Earlier, it changed every few years, and now it evolves every few weeks. When I started working, I used a fax machine and then a clunky computer that slowed me down more than helping me. And now everything is conducted via phones that talk to you.

Within five years of running Peepul, between New York and Mumbai, I began to think of how I would lead its transition between life stages. Very simply put, when you are a boutique set-up, you have a couple of options—

either you get acquired by a larger one; the founder builds a succession plan; or you dissolve the business at a point that feels right to you. For me, creating a succession plan made sense, and I came to this conclusion after much deliberation and many conversations with people I look up to. What was very important for me is to recognize and build on the fact that Peepul is about the team and not just me, which is a reality. But I didn't want to build this the conventional way, that is, hire a head for the company or promote one person to a managerial role (I have just spent too much time with maverick owners).

I wanted to choose a set of senior most team members who would eventually become partners in the business, and I also wanted a representation of different voices and strengths. Initially, it was a diverse group, all with individual experiences and professional ranges, so together they brought in a healthy mix of beliefs and management styles. This was an easy decision to make but difficult to execute, because I took a while to take a step back (and I am still trying). My partners had to build muscles of tolerance, cooperation and management. It was exhausting for all of us to find a way to be on the same page, but over time, we've learnt how to agree, disagree, and call a truce as our values remain similar. I do realise now that future-proofing a firm requires absolute alignment in vision, culture and management. It was exhausting for all of us to find a way to be on the same page, but over time, we've learnt how to agree, disagree, and call a truce. And it helps that our values are all similar.

What people don't tell you enough is that management cannot be improvised. It is a profession on its own and requires rigour, commitment, and lifelong learning. Giving orders is not management, and neither is the schoolteacher approach of monitoring and rewarding people. When I began thinking about choosing my partners and leading the agency through that change, I knew I needed help. Firstly, I wanted to articulate and put into place a clear work culture at Peepul, which allowed everyone to find their voices and niches within a strong, dynamic structure. I knew what the culture was, but

I wanted it to be known to everyone else. Also, personally, I recognised that in order to detach myself and allow others to rise, I needed someone to guide me. After so many years of being in control, stepping back was not going to be easy. And it still isn't.

I decided to hire a coach and was recommended Dr Ruta Vyas by a friend. She works with very large companies but took a liking to Peepul and adopted us. She could see that we needed help and were willing to do the work. Leading forty of us through a workshop across several months and cities, she helped us build a mission statement that worked for us, as a company and not just me or only three other people. We engaged with her for a whole year to build tools, learn new skills, and feel more aligned with one another and the company while remaining diverse. Doing this was one of the best decisions I have made for Peepul, because I see how it has shaped us ever since.

One of my big learnings is that it's important to build a culture that is spelt out. This cannot be a guessing game. There was some amount of dissonance in the people we hired or potential clients who approached us, but once we went through the whole exercise with Ruta, pieces fell right into place and that change translated into how we presented ourselves to the world, both as individuals and a team. This automatically meant that we attracted team members and clients who were on the same page as us. Earlier, if I tried to explain how to behave or how to proceed with a team member, I was often misunderstood or demanding, but once everyone participated in spelling out the company's culture, that is no longer an issue because we have a common set of values that everyone had a part in articulating.

The partners and I have navigated demonetization in 2017, new taxation rules, and the pandemic aside from routine everyday crises and bumps in the road. The fact that we have been able to help one another deal with these situations makes them invaluable to me.

The key lesson I can leave with you right now is that everyone has to define growth for themselves in the context of their business and their bandwidth. While traditional ideas and tried-and-tested methodologies are useful to learn from, the world is changing by the minute, so trust your gut, be in communication with your team (if you have one) and advisors you rely on, and find the path that suits you best. Stagnation or complacency are not options for any of us, but how to fight them is completely your call.

PEEPUL'S COMPASS

Peepul is the leading pan-India brand relations consultancy delivering international standards of servicing driven by passion, innovation and integrity with a personal touch.

MISSION

To provide innovative and effective integrated brand relations solutions which help our clients grow their businesses and realize their marketing goals.

VALUES

Relationship
Integrity
Ownership
Positivity
Learning

A Compass and the North Star

Working with Dr Ruta Vyas was so
transformational for me and my team that
I decided to speak with her, and get some
universal questions answered about management
and leadership. She shares her advice on
and how to navigate growth, expansion and
diversification with your team on board.

What are the key attributes to being a good manager?

First, they must develop the ability to transition out of the
mindset of an individual contributor and start seeing the
value of other team members and what they bring to the
organization. They also need to move out of being a doer and
become a conductor, harnessing the power of people in the
organization, playing to their strengths, creating space for
individuality and eventually being able to step back in order to
let others do their best.

Managers must look at developing three categories of skills -
technical, people and conceptual.

First is the technical aspect. If they are managers, we can assume
they are already knowledgeable, good at execution and have built

expertise in their domain. As they try to scale up, they must involve themselves less in day-to-day tasks and, instead, teach and mentor others, and pass on their technical know-how and know-how to their team members. This will help them free up their time to focus on growing other skills while also developing a pipeline of future leaders for the organization.

Learning to work with people is key for managers. They have to be able to build relationships of trust as well as engage and network with different kinds of people. Learning to influence (even without authority), motivate and inspire others and collaborate, in order to work across silos, is also essential.

Conceptual skills are key for a manager to truly become a leader; to be able to envision the future, innovate, dream, learn, imagine, strategize and be creative. They need to make time to read, learn, listen, travel and think out of the box. This is only possible if managers can get out of the comfort zone (typically their technical domain) and truly leverage the power of the people around them in order to make time for more leadership activities and creative, innovative pursuits.

And would you say that being a good manager is the same as being a good leader?

Certainly not. A manager works transactionally, in a measurable input-output relationship—they focus on tasks, results and performance. A leader works at transformation.

Their input-output is not an arithmetic calculation but is exponential. For 1x unit of input, they can get 10x output. A leader works with people and focuses on the potential, of the organisation and the individuals in it. Management is working with what is available. Leadership works with what is possible. A manager will deliver, but a leader will inspire.

What are your top pieces of advice for people who wish to become good managers and leaders?

1. Think beyond the present. Keep dreaming and innovating.

2. Never think you know it all. Your experience could become more of a liability than an asset if you allow it to inflate your ego and close your mind to learning.

3. Believe that everyone has potential and see the good in others. Appreciate more than you criticise.

4. Manage yourself before you manage others - your temperament, your ego, energy, learning and development, mental and physical health, your self-discipline, ethics and values.

5. Trust the people you work with and have patience while they go through their learning curve.

6. Respect diversity and leverage differences in people without having the same expectations of everyone and without expecting people to be like you.

7. Be flexible and use different styles of leadership with different types of people and for different situations. One size cannot fit all.

8. Above all, treat others with respect, humility and grace.

In the context of how you worked with us at Peepul, what would you tell small business owners about pivoting and expanding?

1. Build your business with a clear vision that outlines what you stand for and what you value. Create a strong culture and the owner must embody every single value himself or herself.

2. Grow the business with personal attention and nurture it lovingly to adulthood, preparing to willingly let go when it is ready to live a life of its own.

3. Nurture talent, spot potential and mentor people who show a bright spark, both intellectually and in terms of values. Build a leadership pipeline and nurture talent gradually and intentionally.

4. As you evolve as a leader, start to delegate and let go. Entrusting and empowering people to make their own decisions, and developing their abilities, thinking and confidence are key. And know that they will never be as "ready" as you would like them to be, but take a chance on your people and let them fly. Mindfully create space for

them as you step back and allow the new leaders to occupy their roles fully.

6. Be there always as an anchor of support, continue to "own" what the company stands for. Don't allow anyone to dilute the brand equity and reputation of the company. Boldly guard against reckless behaviour, unethical actions or decisions that jeopardise the sanctity of the organisation. Remember you've always got to have its back!

How do you help people bring their teams on board with their ideas and vision?

1. We believe that all development and growth must start with insight and so as a first step, we also help the leaders develop a strong and accurate self-awareness. Next, we get them to define what they stand for and what's valuable for them and then create a vision of what they want to see in the future, for themselves personally and professionally. It is important for them to articulate their ideas and vision to themselves first and be extremely clear on the same before they can attempt to being their teams on board. When they are ready to take it to their colleagues, they must take efforts to build a compelling case fuelled by purpose and clarity of the path ahead.

2. Next, they have to learn to listen: to the vision of the people, their ideas as well as their reservations or doubts. There is so much power in that exercise. There is no space for a leader to

think that his or her ideas are the best and that people should naturally align with them. The goal is to build a strong ship collectively, so the team is also committed and the benefits are for everyone.

3. Common goals must be upheld at all times while the leader stays flexible about how these will be achieved. Respecting diversity in people, ideas and methods is vital. Small wins must be celebrated and people must be acknowledged for what they bring to the organization.

4. Staying collaborative is key. Leaders has to learn to navigate challenges, keep an open mind, and develop their own strengths constantly. Continuing to be a learner, and staying open to newer and better ideas that may be different from one's own will keep leaders stay on top of the game and build an organization that is robust, healthy and truly loved by its people, clients and share-holders.

CHAPTER ELEVEN

How to Pivot & Create a Better Brand

I use the word pivot a lot, in conversations with my team and our clients. Nothing highlighted the importance of pivots more than the COVID-19 pandemic, and we've all spent time thinking about the relevance and profitability of what we do and how we can do it better. There has not been a single business conversation I've had that did not include this word and I think that it will continue to be on everyone's minds for some time to come. (I suspect my team makes fun of me, for this and my other weird statements, and look, I am glad they think I am amusing.)

I would personally define a pivot as a logical continuation of the brand, either going further ahead in your current journey or taking a detour to explore a new path. But I want to offer you two more traditional definitions, so here they are.

1

'A pivot means fundamentally changing the direction of a business when you realize the current products or services aren't meeting the needs of the market. The main goal of a pivot is to help a company improve revenue or survive in the market, but the way you pivot your business can make all the difference.

It may be the right time to pivot your business if:

- You can't see much progress even after putting in a tremendous amount of money and resources.
- There is just too much competition.
- The company's progress has plateaued.
- Only one of your company's features or services gets traction.
- Customers aren't responding to your products like you thought they would.
- Your perspective about the industry has changed.'

—Vikas Agrawal, co-founder at Infobrandz, writing in July 2020 for Forbes.com

2

'Pivoting is a lateral move that creates enough value for the customer and the firm to share. Not all pivots result in good business performance. Three conditions are necessary for such lateral moves to work.

First, a pivot must align the firm with one or more of the long-term trends created or intensified [by a current reality].
Second, a pivot must be a lateral extension of the firm's existing capabilities, cementing—not undermining—its strategic intent.

Third, pivots must offer a sustainable path to profitability, one that preserves and enhances brand value in the minds of consumers.'

—Mauro F. Guillén, professor, Wharton School, writing in July 2020 in *Harvard Business Review*

To start off, I chatted with Lulu Raghavan, who has decades of experience working with large and small brands, guiding them through several stages of their journeys. This is the advice she offers: 'Every brand has an opportunity for transformation that would bring it much closer to the customer, further away from competitors and on a journey of constant evolution. It requires taking a long and hard view at yourself currently. The concept of the Johari window from psychology is a useful framework for identity transformation. Keenly understanding how the brand is perceived externally can help to address negatives and bring out more strengths to the forefront. Once the brand is redefined, it is important to use the new meaning of the brand for cultural transformation as well as reimaging the customer journey. The brand must change internally first before changing for customers. Brand transformation executed inside out has more chances for success.'

The point Lulu makes about a brand needing to first initiate change internally is what I spoke about in the previous chapter in the context of Peepul. And I find that as more clients come to us looking for assistance and support in their own pivots, we're able to accompany them on that journey.

The first thing we do is remind the people in charge to reconnect with its DNA. It the brand's important to take stock of its values, how it interacts with customers, the nature of the product and/or service, and its overall goals and priorities. Will pivoting serve all of these? While people automatically assume that pivoting means expanding, that's not always true. We've had several instances of clients coming to us with the expectation that we will help them pivot, treating the word as a synonym of expansion, but when the chips are down, that's not what they want or need, and the whole exercise is a waste of everyone's time.

A number of family-run jeweller brands fall into this category. In one case, a heritage jewellery brand with an impeccable client list and a legacy of over 100 years wanted to scale up because the creative director (who was also of course, part of the family lineage) felt that was what they needed. We did not agree, because we thought their discretion and the fact that you had to visit the main showroom in order to see the jewellery worked in their favour. It created an air of exclusivity that made the brand much more covetable. Eventually, as it turns out, they decided to go ahead with their idea, and it did not work out as they had hoped. And we've seen this play out in a number of ways with other jewellery brands too.

I'm using the example of a certain market, but the cautionary tale applies to everyone. If the strength of your brand is a certain level of confidentiality or personal interaction, you might need to think of pivoting in ways that keep those attributes alive. This is true for restaurants, for fashion brands, and for beauty brands alike.

The COVID-19 pandemic has been a reiteration of our belief in the power of relationships. Human connection, whether face to face or virtual, will never go out of style. Any brand that has recognized this and 'talked' to their stakeholders has set themselves up for implicit trust. The success and sustenance of a brand depend both on agility and how authentically it upholds its values. These factors have helped our clients build strong connections with their human capital—consumers, employees, or service providers. Technology will always evolve, but human connection and relationships will continue to direct the course of business for the foreseeable future. In a nutshell, do less, and do good for good. It's vastly important for brands to meet their consumers—both existing and potential—halfway on the demand-supply spectrum. Social media gives all of us the perfect space to do so. For example: Kama Ayurveda's 'Calm with Kama' playlists take the mindfulness conversation beyond Ayurveda into the realm of sounds that soothe.

BRANCHING OUT

Diversification is, in the luxury and lifestyle space, a very good way to direct a pivot. You can either do it alone or by collaborating with another brand. Take for example Manish Malhotra's collaboration with online beauty platform MyGlamm. To my mind, it is the perfect fit because they relate to one another seamlessly as fashion and beauty. Manish may not have actual beauty credentials, but as a designer, he is conversant with the business; he knows how to work with make-up artists and articulate the looks they must create on models who wear his clothes. And the line balances his brand value of high-octane glamour with the fun and accessibility of MyGlamm. A collaboration works if the brands' DNAs and universes match.

Sabyasachi Mukherjee, whose eponymous brand is iconic, also creates excellent collaborations—in jewellery, homeware, etc.—that feel like seamless extensions of his core values. And Tarun Tahiliani does this too, with his vertical of designing homes with his signature aesthetic.

The primary aim of diversification is to bring you a different kind of customer and add a layer to your brand story that is not achievable otherwise. Global fashion giant H&M, with its collaborations with designers such as Simone Rocha, Karl Lagerfeld, Stella McCartney, Lanvin, etc., is a good case study. With a global audience and a distinct appeal and aesthetic of its own, these limited-edition collections with some of the world's most coveted designers give H&M a chance to surprise and delight its customers. And the designers, for their part, are introduced to a wide and diverse set of customers, many of whom may not otherwise have access to their work or be able to afford it.

CHECKLIST FOR A PIVOT

- Your first 'gut check' should be that your pivot suits your DNA and the ethos of your brand. (How many times have we noticed unnatural extensions to a label? And these rarely work out.)
- Be very sure that whatever you plan to do—collaborate, diversify, go into a completely new direction, or upgrade—it fits into your brand's universe and the long-term goals that you have for it.
- Do not be blown away by a very strong potential commercial opportunity if you know deep inside that it won't sit well with your brand. A customer can tell if a collaboration is forced, so don't take them for a ride. The damage will be too great.
- Sometimes, you just might need to cut your losses and walk away from an unsuccessful move. Do it sooner rather than later.
- Even if your plan feels like you're travelling far away from your core idea, as long as it stays true to brand values, do it. Ask yourself— will this resonate with my core audience while appealing to a new set of people?

CHAPTER TWELVE

What Should
You Do if
Things Go Wrong?

A publicist cannot avoid crises. In my long career, I have seen too many to count, both with my clients and my own company. From a controversial comment to an unpleasant incident, negative market or client feedback, a natural disaster, and now, a global pandemic—we've gone through it all at Peepul. And what helped us navigate each one are quick thinking, deep knowledge, and the ability to keep your wits about you to focus on getting through the storm. In all honesty, in the past twenty-five years, I have represented controversial brands or individuals, signing them up unwittingly, and we learnt as much from them as we have from our other clients. With all of this said, I would break the topic of crisis management down to first having your own house in order and then building the tools to help others.

SAFETY FIRST

To me, values and ethics in business are non-negotiable. How you navigate every aspect of your job—from the confidentiality of clients to handling difficult situations—says a lot about your own moral compass. These beliefs have formed the foundation at Peepul and over the years, through trial and error, we have put in safeguards and practices to make sure we do our best, always. The first and most important thing is to protect the confidentiality of clients and within your own organization. I cannot stress this enough—whether you're a publicist, a content creator, a marketing consultant. Leakage of information is a messy and dangerous matter, and when you work with clients on anything related to their brand or company, it is vital to make sure you are looking out for their interests. From the bottom up, teams need to understand what is at stake if anyone gossips or trades in information. Signing NDAs with clients is standard practice, and at Peepul, we've started asking team members to sign NDAs if they are part of critical discussions with clients and need to handle sensitive information, such as potential business leads or plans at the agency. It is a second line of defence that I feel is much needed.

No one has a perfect sense of judgement, and I will be the first to admit that I have made some bad calls, but I have learnt to keep my ear to the ground and listen to bits of information that come my way about clients or other collaborators. You need to develop a filter to sift through gossip, of course, and have trusted sources that you know have your back. But there is no smoke without fire, so pay attention and use your instinct to make the right call at the right time.

LISTEN, AND LEARN

The first step to crisis management is to be open to feedback and conversation. I cannot tell you how many crises I have dealt with that could have been avoided if people had listened and acted on what they heard. Pre-empting a crisis with honesty, transparency, and the ability to take the long view is always the best way to go. If a client hears valid negative feedback from a customer or any other stakeholder, gets bad press, or has to deal with any other similarly unpleasant situation, our advice to them is always to listen carefully first and do a quick investigation to understand how it happened. This helps you prepare a defence and, if you need to, you can apologize publicly or privately, as is best in that particular instance. This makes the other party feel heard and lets you state your case and end matters in a civil manner. To the contrary, if you find that the feedback or opinion is unfounded, it is best to schedule a meeting and talk things through, presenting your side of the story and finding a middle path so everyone involved is happy and feels validated.

The worst thing to do is bury your head in the sand and either pretend not to listen or hear them out and then do nothing about it. We faced an unpleasant situation with a client years ago, when a team member of theirs caused an injury to a customer and did not make amends. The irate customer, of course, went public with the issue, and we had to deal with the fallout, which caused some serious damage to our client's reputation. It took months of work to walk it all back and reset. What would have saved everything was if the team member had apologized profusely, offered help, and taken charge of the situation. Being overly defensive is never good. This is also why training all team members in crisis management is vital, or every small problem can snowball. Having a PR manual is also an excellent idea, so employees have something concrete and tangible to turn to.

If anything is out in the public domain, first release a statement saying you are aware of the situation, are taking it very seriously, and will offer an explanation within a deadline. This makes it clear that you acknowledge what is happening, which will buy you some time and at least hold your critics at bay.

How you draft this statement is very important, especially today, when cancel culture is rampant. It needs to be sensitive, cognizant of reality, and neutral. The choice of words and the tone in which you write are critical. Do not try to be funny—humour has no place here and will always be misinterpreted. Clear, authentic communication is key. In India, particularly, I've noticed that an apology is almost always dismissed, and the narrative is completely taken over by speculation. Which is why it is even more essential that you keep your head about you, gather the facts, and stick to the truth without being defensive, dismissive, or judgemental. Needless to say, societal and corporate cultural context is equally important—suing or issuing open/public letters may work in another country, but even lawyers will first recommend amicable agreements and settlements here.

What becomes clear very quickly in a crisis is that a company's culture shapes the judgement calls that are made. Are the people in charge willing to listen and apologize? Can they take constructive criticism? Will they allow publicists to help them deal with the matter or do they want to control it themselves? Ideally, a client will be guided both by their own ethics and company policies, and our advice is to integrate the two to arrive at a solution. Also, I always caution clients in fashion, beauty, luxury, or other lifestyle industries that they need to be sensitive to and aware of current political and social circumstances. They cannot afford to ignore the zeitgeist. We had a client release images shot in a state that was undergoing severe political turmoil; the decision was made against our advice and it backfired spectacularly, forcing all of us to spend days on end firefighting.

My intention is not to sound like my team and I are always right or that clients must only and always listen to us. The point is to remember that how you handle a crisis says a lot about what you and your brand stand for and how willing you are to listen to the market. Quick, decisive, sensible action is always the best. Humility and empathy come in good use, always. We live in a social media world right now where anything can go viral at any point, and even if it doesn't, people read comments, they are very focused on reviews, and decisions are now made holistically. So it helps to remember that your customer or potential customer will spend time and money on you if you stay true to yourself.

Reach Across, Make Friends

While I would devour fashion coverage in Paris, I also religiously read fashion reviews every season. I just loved these opinion pieces that taught me a lot about how to look at a runway show from technique to experience. These critiques didn't feel like a personal judgement (even if they were), but seemed to balance out glowing features and advertising budgets with an objective perspective. Because I was still honing my skills in the space, I realized the importance of a good edit, a storied collection, a distinct yet consistent voice and a cut or a silhouette that marked a look or a season. Critiques and reviews are crucial in a media ecosystem, as they ideally only help a brand with a constructive dynamic. They can sometimes make or break a product.

When I was working in New York, I got more and more acquainted with this truth in hospitality—a reviewer coming to a restaurant launch or a hotel walk-through always kept us on pins and needles. Gossip columnists had tremendous influence on reputation and business.

I realized that we were all (secretly or not) obsessed with these pages, and also learnt to accept the symbiotic relationship between stars, publicists, and these columns. We all needed each other.

If you are in a scenario where a journalist wishes to 'leak' out classified intel or personal information, the best way to handle it is to build mutual respect. Think about how it can benefit you or your brand while sharing a chatty piece of news. No one is allowed to cross the line of defamation or misrepresentation, and that remains the subject's prerogative (especially in the US, where you can easily sue). I have tremendous respect for my peers who work in the entertainment space and navigate this dynamic every day.

Move Fast, and Get Help

I turned to Dilip Cherian once again for his expert advice on navigating a crisis. And here is what he had to say.

How does PR help in crisis management? Often, in the lifestyle space, there is very little understanding of why a PR machinery needs to be in place.

Most people who have lifestyle companies believe that they are a)immune from crisis and b)that the agency that is doing their marketing or Instagram can handle crisis. I think if you ask me, you don't need a crisis management agency right from the start but crisis is a function of growth. If you are in a high growth market or highly competitive market, there will be some issue—from customers, on the supply side or regulatory. So not everyone needs a crisis agency but you have to learn how to identify the initial signs of a crisis. You have to be alert and reaching out soon to somebody whose pay grade is higher than soft-selling agencies is a smart thing to do. You have to know when to change gears.

Would you say that there is a formula to managing a crisis? Where do you start?

This is a complex subject but let me try simplifying it.

1. You need to ring fence the size of the crisis—what are the signs of it, and how far can it go? With experience, you know that something can go thus far and no further.

2. Isolate, identify and try to rectify to the extent that you can. If it is an apology, refund or mea culpa, you need to do this early after having thought through the consequences. Don't apologise off the cuff. Pinpoint the source of the crisis and address that. If it has spiralled out of control and now there are people baying for your flesh, you need to make sure you have a certain level of protection. Explain what's happened: this is our defence and this is why we are innocent/not liable.

Given the landscape that you have seen from even five years ago to the social media reality now, do you think crises now escalate more quickly?

Crises have escalated, trigger points are more, there is a cancel culture (your product could get boycotted because of your brand ambassador). Earlier it took a lot of time for a crisis to reach a point that could bother you. The number of flashpoints have increased because of social media. But the advantage also is that you can reach your clients, supporters immediately and directly. There is an outrage a minute so there might be one bigger than yours. You can tell your story at length on your owned media—you don't have to wait for anyone to tell it for you. This is a smart strategy.

Have these new developments changed how you approach this function as an agency?

If you are not the first to change, you are the last to pick up the pieces. We recognised this twelve years ago, and have stepped up listening to what our clients are being talked about. We offer content creation for their owned media. We have influencers on standby to come out and support a client. All of this has grown over the last ten to twelve years. I don't stick to an old formula. Times have changed, and your skills need to change. When we take on a client, we have a crisis protocol that we introduce them to. We train senior management to be prepared. We have non-service people in the team to help out.

Do you think it takes a certain kind of personality to handle a crisis?

I don't think a crisis is anybody's cup of tea. No one can be trained to manage it perfectly. The kind of person who is willing to play American football is different from a graceful gymnast. You need everyone. And not everyone is enthusiastic or competent. Crisis teams need to be small and be supported by people who know the industry being dealt with. The crisis team needs to have a very high threshold for pain and a low threshold for reactivity. They need to be able to see where the fire is, without being choked by the smoke. I don't think it's a disqualification if you cannot handle crisis.

What would you say to someone who finds themselves in a crisis, but cannot spend on hiring a publicist or agency to see them through it?

A crisis should not ferment and froth—the costs are never as high as what the implications might be. Reach out immediately to a professional you can afford. Commit yourself and your best partner to being available to handle it 24/7. Finally, don't expect miracles. Allow the agency to help you ride it out until the crisis is out of your hands.

GROWING ROOTS AND WINGS

Two or three years ago, a fashion designer client of mine had a really fun party at his home, and I learnt about it via the pictures on social media and the gossip columns the next day. The party had gone viral. I hadn't known about it. Neither had my team. We hadn't spoken to the press prior to it. And yet that dinner, attended by Mumbai's A-list, was all everyone was talking about. When I finally got my client on the phone to ask him what sparked the coverage, he said he'd asked his driver to call one photographer, who then spread the word to the paparazzi, who in turn parked themselves outside his residence. In that moment, I really felt like the driver had replaced me as a publicist. It was hilarious, and everyone had a good laugh.

But that's the reality we live in. These days, the game changes every minute, and I don't think there's a rulebook anymore. You are as relevant as your contact list, the likes on your Instagram page, and the number of people who follow you. Are you a part of the right WhatsApp groups? Who DMs you? And when was the last time you were part of something that went viral? (It doesn't matter why you did, only if you did.) So how do you stay in the game?

For the last time, I want to repeat myself—being a publicist has not changed in its essence. It's still about the relationships, doing your best by your clients, and staying agile so you are always two steps ahead. Which is why I think that this industry is a great opportunity for young people to hone their skills—it's about building relationships in a meaningful, non-transactional way, and that's a skill you can use in any field.

The Indian market is dynamic, complex, and demanding. Every aspect of retail is lively and ever-changing, from the malls to e-commerce, to brands that run entirely on social media, and everything in between. Luxury is slowly finding a footing, but its covetability and consumption are unlike any other country in the region. Bridal will always be the biggest market in India—this is a society that spends on weddings, and that is never going to change.

For us, the big shift is that now church and state are one. When I started out, publicists had a powerful role to play in building networks and getting quality coverage for their clients. Today, the journalist's role has changed completely, and editorial formats are no longer what they were. The media works 24/7, and there is the parallel universe of social media and influencers; brands, too, have become publishers of their own content, with access to platforms that allow them to tell their own stories. Because it is increasingly challenging to garner coverage in a non-transactional way, our profession is evolving as well. We are marketeers first and traditional publicists later. When we were asked how we would benchmark our work in a recent call with a potential client, my colleague said, 'Building coverage.' But I chimed in to say, 'We want to make sure your collection sells out this season.' Because that's really the goal now.

To me, this is a very interesting and relevant change. The best publicists have always played a role in brand-building, but now that mandate is open to everyone, and it's grown bigger.

A PR agency is now far more involved in building business for a brand, which gives us a more relevant role than earlier. From working behind the scenes to raising awareness about your clients, we can now step forward and play a greater role, with much more at stake.

The playing field is bigger—publicity now means managing influencers, curating or helping create content, strategizing on campaigns for social media, building collaborations, and having a role to play in events. The plus side is that the ROI is now much more tangible. And having PR absorbed under the marketing umbrella means that the budgets being allocated should be reconsidered, too. It has always surprised me how many clients or potential clients are unwilling to spend on publicity when they are happy to spend on R&D, marketing, branding, events, and so on. You have to give yourself the means to match your ambition, as investing in PR can only make your brand better.

THE NEW PUBLICIST AND THEIR MANDATE

In 2013, we worked with an editor to create a role in the company that we really felt we needed. As brands started creating business pages on Facebook and the manner in which you communicated with the media began to change, we needed help with creating content. Clients required a strong narrative that went beyond a product, a launch, a collection, or even their brand. Journalists were receiving such a wide range of pitches and information that they could not tell one brand apart from the next. Everything depended on how creative we got with the narratives we built and how we presented them. It was the make-or-break point which determined whether an editor or writer would even look at our email or press release. So we collaborated with an editor to come in and consult with us on how to get better at communication skills and ideating—we now had to learn to think in different mediums, and not just print.

Less than a decade later, a publicist's job is now a hybrid between print, digital, and old-fashioned PR. You have to think about content (short and long-form), narratives, social and traditional media, digital storytelling, and entertainment. More than ever, we are a brand's gatekeepers and storytellers. This is why clients must treat their publicist or agency as someone who is part of the larger team. Sign NDAs if you must, but empower them with information. When PR is the last thing on your list, your publicist gets that message, and it can be difficult for them to act in your best interest if they know that their work is not a priority for the company. Building a relationship of trust always helps. I find that I have done my best work for clients who have been open, generous, and collaborative. Especially now, when as a PR agency, my team and I can do everything from engineering collaborations, to helping edit collections and curating events.

To be in this business, you have to like people and be curious. That goes without saying. The relationships you build determine your professional value, and you have to be able to look beyond the transactional aspect. As much as you can, build relationships that are more rooted and meaningful. This is not going to happen with every person, but even in associations that are purely professional, do your homework. I always tell new team members to spend time researching the people they are going to call. If it's an editor or a writer, for instance, have all the information you need about where they have worked, what they do now, what they write about, etc. When it comes to clients, we insist that everyone on that account has researched all press coverage so far, read the materials that they share with us, and has enough know-how about the industry or business they are in. There is nothing sloppier than a publicist who does not know their own client.

The other point that goes hand in glove with people skills is a service mindset.

Ultimately, a big part of PR is about making your clients feel like they are being taken care of. This is often misunderstood as being a yes-woman or yes-man or pandering to them. I totally disagree. We do not pander to our clients, and neither are we afraid of disagreeing with them, sometimes vociferously so.

At Peepul, what I expect from myself and my team is a culture of looking after our clients, much like luxury hospitality. We make it a point to make sure their experience of working with us is always pleasant and professional at the very least. We have to like them and vice versa, because that makes the relationship easier. There have been times when a client has had a problem with a decision we made or how we handled something, but we were all able to work through that because they knew that we care about them, always.

As a publicist these days, I feel like you also have to be able to multitask and have a wide range of interests and an entrepreneurial mindset, even if you are working for someone else. A KRA or a mandate that someone else hands you is no longer enough. The people that we are drawn to hiring are those who want to make things happen and take initiative beyond what is expected of them. Cookie-cutter creativity just does not work anymore. You need to spend time upskilling via online or other courses, reading, listening to podcasts, conversing with your network, etc. Essentially, you must do what you need to in order to stay ahead of the curve. Your ultimate KRA is to add value to your client's universe. If you represent a designer, you need to always have ideas in your pocket: can you introduce them to a jewellery designer to collaborate with? Or a homeware brand? Should they work on a podcast or an editorial collaboration? Think ahead, always.

DRAW A LINE

As much as I love what I do, public relations is a very stressful industry to work in. In many ways, the industry in India is a bit softer and a lot less demanding than it is in the west. In both Paris and New York, it was routine for me and my colleagues to work eighteen-hour days, and up to a point in my life, I never felt there was anything wrong with that. My work drove me, and I wanted to do as much as I could, even though I was not earning enormous amounts of money. I was driven more by what I was achieving and learning. The idea of work–life balance did not exist then, so I suppose I did not know to question my hours or what was expected of me at all. Of course I burnt out several times, but oddly enough, that was the norm, as it still is in many ways.

Do I think work–life balance is possible? Not really. I think that each one of us needs to define our boundaries and stick to them.

Over the years, and as my own life changed personally and professionally, I've come to believe that what matters is longevity, which requires you to pace yourself and focus on quality, not quantity. On an ideal day, I like to put my phone aside at 6.30 p.m. and spend time with my family. I like to see friends often and value any chance I get to host a meal or plan a fun activity with people I love. The path I've chosen for myself and my agency—to stay boutique—fits in with these priorities. And I try and offer the team the same opportunities.

At Peepul, we don't expect anyone to work even on one Saturday every month. I have learnt not to micromanage my team's time and resources, trusting them to get their jobs done instead. And they do. Whether it's me, the partners, or any other team member, we know how and when to prioritize work. If there is a crisis, all rules are forgotten—weekends, public holidays, or private vacation days have been and will be sacrificed if the need arises. But during a regular week, I believe that smart time management and everyone's own sense of responsibility are enough to get things done smoothly.

There can be that sense of guilt when you take time for yourself. We've all experienced it at some point. I know I do, often enough. But I also know that taking a break, whether that's for three weeks or three days, is vital. Travel is the way for me to recharge, get new ideas, and fall back in love with my work. I am enormously proud of the fact that once a year, my family and I take a long vacation without fail, and we also aim to do as many short trips as we can, planned around weekends and public holidays. My clients tease me about my love for getting on a plane, but it's all in good spirit—they know that work never suffers because my fantastic team has my back and that if needed, I will cut any vacation short to deal with an emergency.

A part of the switching off I am so keen on is that it feeds my creativity and inspires me. Every time I travel, I fuel myself with ideas because I get a chance to see exhibits or visit interesting stores and discover brands that I never would have if I did not stop to look and observe. I also love reading international magazines because there is no pressure on me to check coverage and see if someone else did better than we did!

I constantly encourage my team to set work aside and recharge in whatever way they can, too. We cannot expect to be good at our jobs if the only thing we do is work. I know self-care is an overused term that now borders on a cliché, but it is vital.

I love my indulgences—a massage, getting my hair done, seeing friends for a glass (or three) of wine. There can be a sense that taking time off for yourself is not a great thing to do, but my advice is to get the guilt and pressure out of the way and be confident that this is good for you and your work. Especially doing what I do for a living, I can only look my best at a meeting or an event if I feel my best. No one wants to be around you if you are irritated, shabby, or tired. I love accompanying the team for pitches because we all make an effort to look as put together and stylish as we can. And because this means different things to each one of us, we show up as a natty, eclectic bunch.

Alongside my work and my Peepul family, I also have a home and a personal life that I am devoted to. My daughter is ten, and my husband and I decided in early 2021 to move to Goa from Delhi.

I am a wife and mother, but I am not defined by those roles and have not felt the need to let them take over my life. I am never guilty about going to work.

And my daughter, Dayani—who we call Nimki, because we're good Bengalis and love our nicknames—knows this because she has seen me work all her life. And I include her as much as possible. When she was little, the team would come home for meetings and cuddle her as we discussed strategy and pitches. She came to the office with me very often and knew all of my colleagues by name. They came to her birthday parties, and she has built friendships with them, too. My life is not compartmentalized, and this works for me. I want Nimki to know that women can work, play with their kids, host dinners at home, and spend weekends watching movies as a family and all of it is okay. She is a participant, not a spectator. I believe this is foundational wisdom that I can gift her with: that women can do whatever they want to and have fun along the way.

Finally, some of the biggest lessons I have learnt as an entrepreneur have been the most elemental ones, so here they are:

1. Learn how to handle money. Don't be shy about it or give in to the belief that women cannot deal with it. I feel the most empowered when I sit with my CA and understand exactly what he was talking about. Especially if you own a small business, like I do, being able to talk money is vital.

2. Hire people who complement you and whose strengths offset your weaknesses, and please learn to delegate to them. Yes, I follow up with my team, but I do not think for them. I focus on what I do and let them focus on their work too.

3. Take a stand. Being a jack of all trades runs its course very quickly. And stick to your values while you are at it.

4. Be confident enough to look beyond the trends and focus on the longevity of your business.

5. Always keep your eye on the bigger picture, and think ahead.

6. Find your definition of work–life balance (but do have a life beyond work) so you don't burn out.

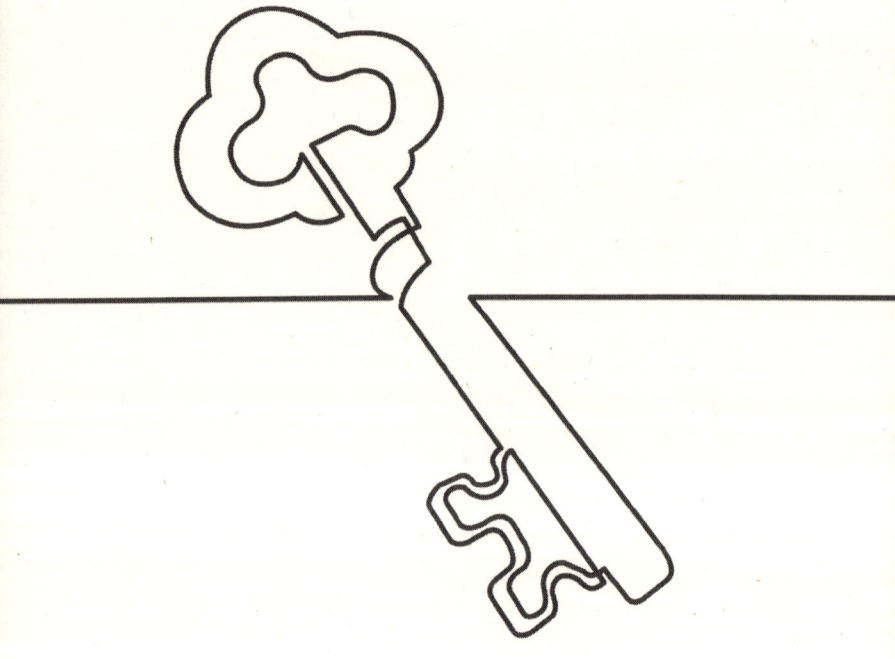

4

Consolidating *your brand* & thinking BIG

CHAPTER THIRTEEN

What Is a Legacy and How Can You Build One?

'Availability and desirability are key tenets of a successful brand. According to Brand Asset Valuator, the world's most comprehensive study of brands, energized differentiation, relevance, esteem, and knowledge are key pillars of strong brands. Differentiation and relevance constitute brand strength. Esteem and knowledge constitute brand stature. Brand strength is a leading indicator of profitability.

'The best brands stand for something distinct. They manifest this meaning of the brand in the entire experience of the brand across all touchpoints. They are relentlessly consistent about the meaning of the brand but they deliver this meaning in fresh and energizing ways.

'Most brands get it wrong because what they promise is miles apart from what they deliver. There is a wide gap between expectation of consumers and what they actually experience. Sometimes it is because the marketing and branding is brilliant and paints a wonderful picture of the brand, much ahead of what it can deliver. Sometimes the execution discipline does not exist. So while the brand strategy may be very sound, it falls apart in execution.

'Legacy is about history, heritage, track record. It is about being special and different. About treating your customers with the utmost care. You can build it by relentlessly delivering value to all your audiences day in and day out. And also taking the time to ensure this value is communicated to your audiences.'

—Lulu Raghavan

As demonstrated by what Lulu says, there are many aspects to legacy. When we talk to clients about it, though, I like to distil it down to a simple question. When your customers talk about your brand five or ten years from now, I ask them, what do you want them to use as a visual cue? For example, when we think about Tiffany, their iconic blue packaging comes to mind. Cartier is synonymous with the Trinity Ring, and Hermès with the Birkin bag. When you say Good Earth, you think of the Mughals. And these are not connections that were made quickly or by spending marketing dollars. Money cannot buy you longevity. What creates legacy is storytelling, consistency, and a very clear DNA that runs through everything you do as a brand. It also helps if your customer feels invested in your brand and its story even if they don't own your product or use your service. Chanel, for instance, is coveted globally by millions, and many of these people may not own a bag or a piece of jewellery made by Chanel but love the brand and are taken with its history and values.

There is also an important social and cultural difference that I want to highlight here. International brands such as Dior, Prada, Givenchy, and Lanvin, to name just a few, are structured very specifically. There is a clear story, visual language that has been layered over the years, and a creative head who takes the brand forward with their vision while staying firmly grounded in its heritage. Every iteration over the decades adds to the legacy and the magic. In India, things work differently, as they often do. An heirloom saree that is passed down through the generations does not necessarily come from a well-known brand, but it has a deep emotional connection. Given the diverse and talented communities of artisans and craftspeople, a lot of what Indians hold dear when it comes to luxury and lifestyle has been handmade, in techniques that have been perfected over decades and sometimes centuries. So in this market, it is safe to say that we look at legacy very differently, and that is an important insight into the Indian consumer's psyche. There are luxury brands in the fashion space, and especially in jewellery, but they are, almost without an exception, family-run.

When clients come to us with legacy on their minds, they expect us to help them find relevance in the current marketplace and work with them to keep their brand's history and heritage alive. Again, these are usually family-run businesses such as The House of Angadi, Amrapali, or Raniwala 1881. They have created a signature product range and have customers who have been loyal to them for decades. What they want is to tap into the zeitgeist and translate their values in a way that they appeal to the contemporary customer.

The first thing we want to do is a deep dive into the brand's DNA and value system. Some clients are eager to skip this, but that is usually a mistake. If you are a brand with a heritage that wants to stay relevant, make sure your

PR partners, whether that's an agency or an in-house team, understand that history very well. One example I would like to share is of The House of Angadi. When we started working together, K. Radharaman, who heads the brand, walked us through its history meticulously and patiently. If he could have taken us to the family's ancestral village, he would have. What this exercise did is make the Peepul team completely familiar with Angadi in a holistic manner. So when we, in turn, talk about the brand, we are confident and invested in the messaging. I cannot emphasise how important this is for a publicist—we are a brand's ambassador, and the responsibility of finding stories to tell lies with us. Half-baked information will not help us do our jobs well.

REINVENTING HISTORY

Once we have all the information we need, we then start thinking about ways in which to tell the legacy story. And there are a couple of go-to methods to do this:

Create an experience that highlights the brand's USP. We suggested to House of Angadi that they take a select group of storytellers and opinion-makers to Kanchipuram to visit temples and looms, connecting the dots between heritage, craft and design. Apart from being a great experience, it also allows people to understand the provenance of the brand, what makes it unique, and help them ideate about the stories they want to tell. Similarly, for the twenty-fifth anniversary of Tarun Tahiliani's brand, we opened the doors to his factory, which is quite unusual for an Indian company to do. What we wanted was to introduce people to the artisans and the painstakingly detailed work they do. It also communicated the fact that the brand truly values its craftspeople and is confident enough to let you see what happens behind the scenes.

Showcase the brand's DNA. Good Earth curated an iconic exhibit at the V&A Museum in London in October 2015, and this was a beautiful way of showcasing the brand's legacy. Internationally, Dior and Alexander McQueen have created much-acclaimed exhibits that have people queuing up. What this exercise does is validate the brand's influence and showcase it in a larger context.

Another way to do this is to bring the provenance into the brand's communication in a poignant way. We advised our client Raniwala 1881 to shoot a campaign in their ancestral home in Beawar. The structure was dilapidated and they were hesitant, but our idea was clear. It was important to differentiate our client from every other jewellery brand in Jaipur, and there is a lot of clutter there. While everyone uses Jaipur as a brand attribute, shooting in that home established Raniwala's legacy and roots and ensured that they own that space and that story.

'Being a part of a legacy, and a family business is a blessing because of the level of experience and knowledge that is shared. As a brand, we work with a balance of both the orthodox and the modern avenues of business. Initially, our approach was driven by the experiences of our older family members as the jewellery business is built on relationships fostered over generations. Later, we shifted towards the B2C segment as we realised the need of the market and our trust in the potential of Jadau as a craft. While being a part of the industry, we took forward the step to create and take ahead the legacy of the craft and our family,' says Abhishek Raniwala, director, Raniwala1881. 'For us at Raniwala, our belief in the craft, and the fact that every piece is handmade by craftsmen who have generations of experience is very strong. Our designs are ethno-contemporary and the pieces we create that place a historical craft in a modern context have become very popular with today's customer.'

Create an emotional connection. Especially in India, occasions matter, which explains why the bridal and wedding markets are as large as they are. Family connections matter since this is a culture that treasures heirlooms.

Build thought leadership. One of the essential things to do in order to build a legacy is to start having conversations beyond the product, people or the company's name, for the greater good of the industry. It is a way for you to showcase your expertise in the domain. For example, Rajiv Arora and Rajesh Ajmera, the founders of jewellery brand Amrapali, have always collected pieces that interest them and have historical or cultural value. In 2018, they founded the Amrapali Museum in Jaipur, which showcases their incredible collection of Indian jewellery and jewelled objects. While the museum and their brand have jewellery in common, the purpose of the former is to share a passion with the world.

HOW DO YOU BUILD LONGEVITY?

If you're an entrepreneur who is new to brand-building or you have a young brand, it might be too early or too overwhelming for you to think about legacy. What does help, though, is to keep sight of the attributes of a legacy brand and bake them into your story as you go:

- Build trust with your consumer.
- Be clear in your storytelling.
- Stay authentic and honest.
- Own your narrative.
- Build an emotional connection with anyone who interacts with your brand.
- Find ways to give people a piece of your story—add a little booklet to every package, or even a monthly email newsletter helps.

Something Old, Something New

K. Radharaman is the CEO and head of design
at House of Angadi, and he steers the legacy
brand into the modern world with one eye on
tradition and the other on innovation. I could
think of no one better placed to talk about how
to stay true to a heritage brand's roots, while also
creating new stories to tell.

'The House of Angadi is a unique entity in that it was founded
by me only in 2001 even though my family had been involved
in textiles for 600 years. This meant that I inherited a legacy
but not a company. It was therefore a deliberate choice on
my part to adhere to the values of my forefathers in the way I
conceptualized and managed the business.

I believe that there are some core business values that define
a business. These will shape the business and define its legacy
for succeeding generations. The core values that shaped our
business were always based on the underlying principle that
we were custodians and *not* owners of society's wealth. This
principle motivates our every action, and in turn these values
enable us to act and think differently. They drive us to think
long term and build brands that will hopefully outlive us and
will serve a larger purpose than merely enriching their owners.

There are many different aspects to the legacy I inherited. It consists of an unrivalled mastery of weaving, an understanding of the vocabulary of design, and a spirit of innovation that saw our family pioneer many firsts in the history of Indian textiles.

These were all part of the lessons I learnt from my father, grandfather and other elders in the family. The ones I chose to imbibe and act upon are those I think were at the core of their philosophy of doing business and are therefore beyond compromise.

Staying true to the values of a business cannot come at the expense of economic viability—which is, at the end of the day, the core function of a business. Conversely, financial goals cannot undermine the philosophy and core values of a business entity. Striking this balance is the biggest challenge for all modern businesses. This explains why it is important for every heritage brand to keep reinventing itself without tampering with its DNA.

The core values of a business cannot enslave it blindly to past practices. It is important for brands to constantly reimagine their business practices and to acquire new capabilities.

It is necessary to emphasize here that the choice of business practices cannot be an exercise in superficiality but needs to be a deep and meaningful act that can only be carried out through long-term thinking, unwavering commitment to core values, and audacity of vision.

I believe that the greatest challenge in the Indian context is not to build a business of scale, but to build a business which marries scale, quality, and innovation. Each of these three attributes have the power to collectively and individually enrich not only a business but also the society and environment in which it operates. And therefore, in an ideal world, achieving one of the outcomes cannot and must not be at the expense of the other. At the risk of subscribing of committing oneself to perfectionism—this is the Holy Grail that we pursue at The House of Angadi.

The key is to retain the brand's core values and indeed amplify them to make it relevant to a contemporary audience. Understanding what makes it unique is essential to positioning the brand appropriately, and this requires an in-depth analysis of a brand's strengths, credibility, and shortcomings in equal measure.

In the long term, this can mean creating entirely new vehicles for brand messaging, and while this can be a time- and cost-intensive exercise, it is the approach that works best for brands such as ours.

Every brand activity today can be leveraged on social media to optimize its positioning and reach. Social media tools and platforms are slowly acquiring critical mass in India, and the convergence of the platforms with traditional media presents opportunities across the spectrum.

While traditional media shall still remain the first port of call for many brick-and-mortar and luxury brands, social media plays an invaluable role in amplifying the brand message in a cost-effective manner. So while brand deliverables continue to remain offline in many cases, the brand promise and experience has become omnichannel (Lexico approved) or omni-channel in virtually all but a few cases.'

Building a Brand with a Culture

I have mentioned Chandon several times in the book for the way in which the brand created a culture of sparkling wines in India. For a detailed perspective on how they achieved that, I turned to Sophia Sinha, marketing head, Moët Hennessy India.

'Everyone builds brands but only few create a culture. A culture is something that becomes an intrinsic part of your daily life, defines your habits, speaks about who you are and is passed on. Which is why building brand culture is not easy at all but the challenge makes it fun.

To be iconic, you either become an idelible part of culture or create your own. To do any one of these, you need to really get into the psychology of the consumer, and tap into their desires, wants and needs. Even if they don't know that they need something, you will know that they do. This is where consumer insight and mapping occasions and trends come into play. Marketing is both an art and science. Unfortunately the art takes precedence for most brands which is why there are few iconic brands. Most don't use foresight and trend mapping.

At Chandon India, I have spent nine years learning about my consumer. This journey didn't start when we launched the brand but before The stop is throwing off grammatical structure, rephrase as either 'before we did, taking a' or 'before we did. It involved taking...' taking a deep dive into understanding the route to market, accessibility of products, market dynamics and then finally watching a team observing consumers before spending a lot of time talking to consumers. Which I still do. It's not about focus groups, which I don't see as the only option any longer. It's about talking to people wherever you are and learning on the go. I also spend hours online researching, and following trendsetters, and global influencers. Reading tons of books and talking to my colleagues across the world to understand what is happening globally is also important. We are no longer seven billion people across seven continents. We are seven billion people across thousands of digital platforms. And we are all connected.

If you have your hand on the pulse, you have the foresight and insight to do what you need for your brand. Did we always get it right? Hell no! I got seven out of ten things wrong when we launched because we were the first to try anything. However, one thing we did well was to stay agile and work really fast. We didn't have time to waste so we had to keep making changes to be able to get it right. It also helps to have people behind you backing your vision and passion. I lucked out there with Moët Hennessy.

Once you get foresight and insight, it's about execution. At Moët, we believe in creating and providing an experience.

are believers in experience. It doesn't matter what we do, we won't do it until it meets LVMH standards. So we sacrificed ideas that were easy wins and chose the road less travelled - no discounts, no cheap activations, no "save the penny" attitude. Every activation or promotion we have done has become a benchmark within the alco-bev space. Every one of them. Because we were patient and refused to compromise on quality just to get quantity.

'Passion also helps you keep going. I mean, imagine building a sparkling wine brand in a whisky market! It's unheard of. It took guts and passion coupled with patience and hard work. One needs to understand that overnight success is actually a thing to be scared of, because you haven't failed. At Chandon we bruised ourselves but got back up again. I was clear from the beginning that we were not launching a brand, we were here to build a culture. Period.

Have we done it? I would say, yes it is taking shape. Did we ever think that Indians would open bottles of bubbly at their celebrations and then drink it? Who knew that brunches, lunches, cocktail hours and dinners would see flutes in people's hands? But it is happening. And we are only at the tip of the iceberg. There is so much more to come.'

CHAPTER FOURTEEN

How Do You Translate Your DNA Playbook into the Zeitgeist?

When we work with a legacy brand that is looking to build relevance in new forms and channels, our priority is to help them capture a narrative that can be shared with old champions and new stakeholders, who can then amplify it.

We want to be able to share the story of the brand, the people behind it, and its new direction. When we sit our clients down with the tastemakers—editors, influencers, reviewers—we want to immerse them in the universe of the brand. Personally, I am not a fan of large formats such as press conferences and prefer getting my clients to have intimate, personal conversations with people so there is room for engagement and a true exchange of ideas with a like-minded stakeholder. And senior editors and reviewers also prefer one-on-one conversations because they can be more valuable. But as you know by now, I am a huge fan of crafting experiences that share the brand's ethos.

So how does one remain relevant as a legacy brand? Start with a meaningful message that will appeal to your existing consumer as much as to an increasingly young and aware audience. Change never happens overnight, but how do you keep pace with a globalized digital audience? You follow their path if it's aligned with your DNA. And taking a stand usually helps. Think about who your brand ambassadors and friends are and whether you are building on a conversation or starting one.

It is believed that designer Coco Chanel's universe was fuelled by art, music, and literature. When the brand Chanel decided to team up with Princess Charlotte Casiraghi of the royal family of Monaco, it was not only because of the world's fascination for royalty, but also because she could conjure a side of Coco Chanel's literary interests by starting a literary salon. It is a clever way to immerse the Chanel customer and admirer into the iconic brand's intimate and mysterious world.

At Peepul, we like planning for long lead-ups so that there's time to tell good stories. Sometimes it takes us six to nine months to plan a launch, and I caution against rushing this because the lead-up is as important as the launch itself. You want to first study the zeitgeist, your new market, and your potential customer and get comfortable with what it is and who they are. This takes time in order to be authentic. There are no CliffsNotes to this process.

I've already said that I overuse the word 'pivot', and another word I find myself and my team using often is 'democratizing'. What we mean by this is that a luxury and/or heritage brand has to approach a new, and often larger, segment of customers in order to stay relevant and to evolve. Diversification is key to a legacy brand. One of the blessings and curses of these brands is that they can expand to new markets and acquire younger customers, but how they choose to do both can be challenging. As an agency, it becomes our responsibility to keep cool hunting for people who fit the values of the brand.

We always talk to brands about the story they want to tell. It is important to never compromise on brand values, because you are reinventing for a reason and not erasing your past. The conversations and stories you create will guide the journey into a new market, or with new customers.

Swarovski is a favourite example of mine. A brand with a larger-than-life global legacy entered the Indian market and found a way to talk to this fairly complex and diverse audience. By creating clever collaborations, working on products that really resonate with the local market while maintaining global guidelines, and putting a huge push on their jewellery, which is always a hit with Indians, Swarovski has managed to become a part of routine conversation. It is at once aspirational and accessible. The brand DNA is untouched, but by tightening and focusing their messaging, they have both mass appeal and are 'masstige' in a sense. With stores at airports, crystals on sarees, and capsule collections, they are accessible and coveted.

When a legacy brand goes local, it's always a bit of a gamble. Hermès, the iconic luxury house, known for its richly coloured scarf designs, sought to boost its presence in India with a limited-edition sari, which was priced in line with the brand's other comparable products. I have to say that as a sari lover, I thought it was a brilliant idea. A dear friend of mine bought a piece, and I could see why. It was a collectible. But does the exclusivity tag work in India? I am not sure. So as *Forbes India* wrote at the time, 'How well the Indian market will respond to the French couturier's offering is anyone's guess.'

STAYING RELEVANT

From a legacy standpoint, there is one brand that I feel let down by—the iconic Ambassador car, which is now close to extinction. When I moved to India, I had the chance to buy a second-hand Ambassador (which is painted hot pink, if you please). You'd be surprised (or not) to know that the Ambassador gained a lot of attention from diplomats and expats who perhaps saw it as a relic from bygone times. This car has actually oddly enough 'branded' me and frankly needs no PR. It makes people smile on the streets and just generally is a showstopper.

Sadly, Hindustan Motors stopped manufacturing its famous Ambassador after a few failed attempts to revive it, sometime in 2014. I was one of the last perhaps to buy a second one, in 2013. To me, it reminded me of my summer holidays in Calcutta and brought many memories along with it. I never understood why a car with such a storied journey and romance never made it. The definition of comfort and branding changed, and unfortunately the Ambassador couldn't keep up with our times, and so its manufacturing was ceased.

Stand Up, and Be Counted

Revitalising legacy brands is not easy or quick work, but it can be done. And, one might argue, it needs to be done. The person I turned to for advice on this subject was my friend, Parmesh Shahani, author of the bestselling book *Queeristan,* founder of the award-inning Godrej India Culture Lab and a globe-trotting public speaker and consultant on LGBTQ rights in India.

I want to first talk to you about your personal brand and the multiple hats you wear—across academia, business and the creative industries. Can you tell me how and why you do this?

Why I do this is because of two reasons. The first is my unique set of experiences—I spent my 20s running an internet startup, working with newspapers like the *Times of India*, magazines like *Elle* and even on a film set. The second is my education. Most people go from theory to practise, but in my case, I went from being a media practitioner to a student, when I joined MIT in 2003, and the ethos of my program there, that of applied humanities, was something that I fundamentally resonated with. What is the role of the humanities in solving some of our world's greatest challenges?

With regard to the personal brand question, I have always enjoyed doing multiple things. And who says that you can't sit in the front row at fashion week one day, while simultaneously working on something that others might deem more serious on another? I think in today's world, multi-dimensionality is being more and more valued and my personal brand is very much about this.

Working for a legacy brand is both an honour and quite challenging in a changing landscape. Could you share a bit about your experience with Godrej and other large groups?

The process of how I joined Godrej was interesting. I had a vague idea called the India Culture Lab, and starting talking to different people about it. Via common acquaintances, I was connected to Nisa Godrej, chairperson and managing director, Godrej Consumer Products Limited. After a long day of wonderful conversations, Nisa asked me to work for the firm. I agreed to only if she would help fund the India Culture Lab idea. Which she did and I joined Godrej in late 2010.

Godrej is a legacy brand—more than a hundred years old. And so it is challenging to innovate on how to create something fresh and new while at the same time staying rooted in your past. For me to bring about the changes I did, I decided to tap into Godrej's deep roots in values as a pivot around which I could frame a lot of my radical ideas—as a bridge towards a brighter future. I proposed that all of my ideas would help Godrej bridge the past and future. Godrej should support them because it would be a very Godrej thing to do—to champion the idea of Indianness, as a company rooted in the swadeshi movement, but also as an inroad into the future ahead.

When I came up with the India Culture Lab idea, I wanted to cross-pollinate different kinds of conversations about modern India. After I joined Godrej in 2010, I began to develop the structure to enable such cross-pollination. With a small but sufficient budget for our operations, our Lab did many different things during the decade of its existence—it went on an indefinite sabbatical post Covid. Firstly, even though we were funded completely by Godrej, we imagined ourselves as a public resource and not as a private entity and operated independently within the Godrej setup.

What conversations were not being had about contemporary India? We tried to work at the intersection of these issues by curating public events on the Godrej campus in Vikhroli Mumbai, across different formats. Some could be talks and lectures while others might be performances or even pop-up museums, like the ones we built around the issue of migration in June 2019.

In parallel with our public events, we ran a small two-part educational program that aimed to tap into students at the undergraduate and graduate level across India and outside. We ran a small leadership training program just for humanities students in Mumbai and we also offered fellowships to humanities students from across India and other countries. We gradually became interested in map-making and resource-building for wider publics. We made a map of 200 cultural institutions across Mumbai before we went on sabbatical, and we often assembled cultural practitioners from across the country to see how we might all be able to collaborate better.

I am proud that we created an example of how an entity can sit in between different worlds—and create value. I firmly believe that hyphenation and translation are going to be key elements of the world of tomorrow. Perhaps these are going to be the spaces where solutions to some of our country's most vexing issues will come from? Our Lab existed as one such liminal space and I hope that its decade-long success might impact the intellectual landscape of India, in many small ways, over the years to come.

I also want to mention here that in any project, you are only as good as your collaborators. During my journey at Godrej, I helped many internal teams—like corporate communication and others. So when the actor Aamir Khan was our brand ambassador and visited Godrej in 2013, I went out of my way to help the team, and even hosted a talk with him to ensure its success and in return they always went of their way for me.

You have made a trailblazing case for LGBTQ inclusion in the corporate world—can you tell us about how you worked towards this change?

First of all I am so proud that over the years, we have accomplished a lot on the policy front at Godrej with regard to LGBTQ inclusion. From starting with basic non-discrimination, to paying for a same-sex partner's health insurance, to having a gender-neutral adoption policy, to replacing the word 'spouse' with 'partner' across communication and documents, the changes have happened slowly and steadily and most of these changes took place in an India in which Section 377 was back on the books, courtesy the Supreme Court decision of 2013. We launched our landmark Godrej Gender Affirmation Policy in 2019. It stated that employees wanting to undergo gender transition could claim up to Rs 5 lakh of a one-time reimbursement for non-cosmetic surgeries and Rs 60,000 per annum for hormone replacement therapy. In the same year we announced the creation of two all gender washrooms at our Godrej One headquarters in Mumbai.

How did all this happen? First, the impetus from the top. I cannot overemphasize just how important it is for senior leaders to lead inclusion initiatives. The second is that over the years, our Lab and collaborations have created the right framework for change. I think that one of our Lab's biggest successes has been in creating a conducive environment for the message of LGBTQ inclusion to spread deep into

Godrej. Over the past decade we must have hosted a 100 LGBTQ themed events which were attended by Godrej employees in addition to the general public over the years.

Also, we used our Culture Lab to collaborate extensively with other organisations. For instance in 2017 we partnered with the UN to launch the global standards of LGBTQ inclusion in India. This event that took place on October 12, 2017, created history. For the first time in our country, there were about 100 business and HR leaders from leading companies like Hindustan Unilever, Procter & Gamble, Tata Sons, Accenture, SAP, Ikea, Intuit, Mahindra & Mahindra, Aditya Birla Group, and many others, all gathered together in a room, asserting their support for LGBTQ rights. All these leaders unequivocally agreed that LGBTQ rights are human rights and that they would push for change in their respective organizations.

I believe that the secret sauce to my success inside Godrej with regard to LGBTQ inclusion is the combination of things that we have catalysed. If we just had policies and strong leadership backing LGBTQ issues at Godrej, but no Culture Lab and global collaborations, it wouldn't have worked as well. If we just had policies and culture but no leadership thrust from the top, it wouldn't have been so good either.

I have no qualms in sharing with you, and you will appreciate this since you're from PR, is that one of my strategies over the years has been to get as much press as I can for my work, and I use the press coverage as a lever to push for the change I desire. I strongly believe that the press writing about Godrej as an inclusive company actually convinced a lot of people within Godrej to act inclusive, and the press coverage certainly helped in establishing Godrej as one of the early movers on the LGBTQ inclusion scene in India, and opened the doors for other companies to follow.

How does taking a stand with a strong message change a brand dynamic from within and then in the public eye?

The world has changed. Customers and employees have changed. If you don't take a strong stand—you are like an ostrich with your head in the sand, or like a dodo. You will become irrelevant very, very soon!

A brand can no longer afford to be neutral. Brands, and the organizations behind them, need to take a stand. So much good public advertising over the years, from brands big as well as small, with regard to LGBTQ inclusion has come about because the brands have taken a stand. Globally, too, being authentic is something brands supporting LGBTQ issues are cognizant of. Also, how a brand responds to negative publicity is also key in this regard. In today's world it is clear that as a brand you need to stand up speak up and show up for your queer customers and employees—they expect it of you and in return, they will reward you with their talent and business.

It is important here, and I can't stress the fact enough that your
engagement needs to be genuine. So as a brand when you are
taking a strong message publicly it is vital you support this
with doing the groundwork within your own organisation. If
you are putting up pride month posts and doing Instagram
Live with influencers, you better have your own policies in
place and treat your own employees well, otherwise you will be
called out for your pinkwashing. In tomorrow's world, only the
truly authentic will survive and thrive!

ALL TOGETHER NOW

Collaborations are a fantastic way to revitalise a brand, take it in a new
direction and/or attract a different kind of customer. For publicists,
collaborations provide the impetus to be experimental, manage interesting
conversations, and accompany a client on an important journey. There are
many reasons why brands decide to collaborate, but if we were to generalise,
an association between two brands helps each of them explore new avenues,
reach out to one another's target audience, and experiment in a fairly
non-risky manner. If engineered correctly and with enough thought, a
collaboration is great fun all around.

The designer Sabyasachi Mukherjee, for example, decided to
partner with French kindred spirit in the couture space, the talented and
whimsical Christian Louboutin (whose heels can kill you but you can kill
for, too). Both couture makers associated in the making of limited-edition
footwear for Louboutin's twenty-fifth anniversary. Christian Louboutin
brought Sabyasachi's workmanship to the world beyond the sari and

lehenga, while he was also able to cater to the Indian market with a gem of a boudoir in his store in Mumbai that would be for brides. Both have pursued many further successful association at landmark moments with critical acclaim and sales success. Such inventive associations are unique and essentially fuel new audiences and reignite conversations beyond the business footprint.

Pareina Thapar, who represents Sabyasachi and works closely with him, spoke to me about how the designer constantly injects new ideas into his eponymous brand—'Sabyasachi has a clear vision to build a global luxury brand from India. He is a long-term thinker who has sharp clarity of vision. Having a strong creative voice, an entrepreneurial spirit and the ability to understand business realities is rare. Sabyasachi has plotted the path of his brand carefully, and he builds teams that reflect the brand values and then empowers them to execute his vision. Legacy is not built in the short-term.'

Building New Worlds

Gucci has been incredible at building inventive associations which have magnified the brand in staying not only relevant, but living through disruption. My dear friend Maneka Thadani, marketing and communications manager at Gucci, shares her thoughts and insights on the cycles a brand goes through. I was interested in her personal perspective as she has worked with the brand since its entry in India.

Working for a legacy brand is both an honour and quite challenging in the new reality. Could you share a bit about your experience with this?

It's been twelve years and counting that I have been working with Gucci. My first luxury purchase was from the brand, and it was definitely a job I was super excited to take on.

Although I had already been in the industry for over eight years prior to my taking on this role, the level of learning and personal growth I have had working for Gucci has been incomparable. Interacting with the best in the industry and being fortunate enough to call many not just colleagues, but friends; working with regional teams and gathering insights on the luxury industry across global markets; and of course having access to the best minds in the business and key learnings across innovation, product planning, strategy, and marketing.

As I was one of the foremost employees in India, it was great to be able to be a part of an extremely small team that was setting up the business, thereby giving me insights and learnings into various aspects apart from just my own role.

We continue to work with a small team which can sometimes be challenging, but the advantages include strong and constant communication and learnings across departments, giving you a holistic and multidimensional approach to the business, which is extremely important when building and formulating brand strategy.

Working with a small team also means it taught me how to pretty much handle all aspects of branding and communication, be it PR, strategy, VIP and influencer marketing, advertising, or events.

What are the key lessons one can learn from a legacy brand when it comes to storytelling and communication?

I think the most important thing is the constant need for innovation and growth. The way to build strong narratives that are unique and most importantly resonate with the brand values.

This also includes innovation not just in terms of storytelling in itself, but also in terms of platforms. It is important to embrace technological changes and avenues around us and use them to reach a larger global audience.

How do you approach local messaging within the parameters of the international universe of the brand?

As a global brand, we are always constantly working on innovative and exciting projects.

While it is extremely important to communicate what the brand is doing globally, it is also important to find a way to integrate locally. I am fortunate enough to be able to work with teams that have really trusted me. I have been able to work on some unique ideas and deliver an unusual strategy over the years.

You are very proficient in identifying the right people to work with and the most striking collaborations. Would you have any advice or tips to share about how to do this?

Primarily you have to understand the brand and the core values it stands for. Thereafter, it's about identifying people who resonate with those values and the brand aesthetic. This makes the narrative truly authentic. Over the years, as a result, we have built some great long term relationships and added to our diverse community, our very own #guccigang.

As a brand, we have always championed inclusivity, authenticity, and ingenuity. A large part of our global community has always been about engaging with young and new talent, being able to join hands with different voices across various creative fields, exploring subcultures, but most importantly about challenging embedded norms.

Personally, I also enjoy being on the pulse of things. I have a constant thirst for knowledge. I think staying curious is incremental to our jobs.

I love a challenge, the challenge to innovate . . . I love to go down the path less trodden, I love to be the first to be able to tell a story.

Media, PR, and brand communication were changing much before COVID-19, but the pandemic has accelerated that and changed all the rules. What do you see as the new trends emerging?

Changing media landscapes in the wake of the pandemic have caused a complete shift in our ecosystem. We need to adopt a 360-degree approach as a result which is not limited to traditional media but also includes digital collaborations with influencers, product seeding, and multimedia content.

The key focus should be on deeper and more engaging and contextual storytelling, invoking desire through visual narratives, and the importance of going beyond reach to real engagement.

Lastly, insights and analytics are key to knowing if you are on the right track. Share of voice, earned media value—these benchmarks will be the way forward to understand the measurement and impact of our work on the business.

BEGINNER'S MIND

Before I hand over you to the brilliant insights that pepper the last section of the book, I wanted to share my own thoughts about my profession and the current landscape. The truth is that through my career—twenty-five years and counting—I have been told so often that I 'pay compliments because I am in PR'. It always upsets me, and I feel insulted personally and on behalf of my industry because PR is not about being schmaltzy. Or spinning a story. Or, I'm just going to say it, being phony. It is a serious profession that requires a diverse skillset that not many have, and the work we do is artful and very essential. (As for the compliments, I am just a nice person!)

When I set out to write this book, my primary goal was to demystify PR, and everything else got added in along the way, to set a context for you. I hope it's been helpful, and that you feel like you have a companion as you navigate the new landscape of relations for your brand and understand the purpose of public relations. Whether you are an entrepreneur or a publicist, I've written this for you. And if you appreciate or value our profession a tad more, my mission is accomplished.

What I would love is if public relations professionals came together to shed light, as an industry, on the benefits of PR and how it can elevate your business and your brand. Because what we do is even more relevant today. Unfortunately, the lack of governance in the lifestyle PR space doesn't help, especially in India and similar markets. In several countries, the business is more established and there are software systems that help build databases, provide analytics, and track coverage. All of these make the work we do more tangible and valued. In the finance and the technology worlds, regulations and guidelines shape the best practices of the profession. We need more of all of this in lifestyle PR in India.

And this is a good time to think about it because as I write this book in 2021, there is so much disruption around us and PR is being forced to evolve. India is following in the footsteps of many other countries as print media slowly shrinks and the digital landscape takes over with the rise of many new players. Large corporates and privately owned digital platforms launch something new every month. Platforms such as Beautiful Homes, owned by Asian Paints, or The Voice of Fashion, run by RISE Worldwide, Reliance's lifestyle arm, are just two examples. And independent platforms keeping mushrooming by the minute—from Tweak India, founded by Twinkle Khanna, to Arts of Hindostan, which seems on its way to become one of the rising voices in arts and culture. The consumer is toggling and juggling and perhaps now struggles with picking which platform to follow and which to trust. Added to this are the influencers (from macro to micro and nano).

So where does PR fit in?

According to me, our function follows the path of the consumer. And so today, our contact lists have shifted towards these new audiences and targets, which are mainly digital and range from a large platform to a micro-influencer. What does this mean for the New Age publicist? The reach is simply far wider, multi-channel and location-agnostic.

My biggest dream is finally coming true—I can live in India and reach out to digital platforms wherever my client wishes to be, whether that's Paris, New York, or Milan. (Yes, I believe in world domination.) The publicist's new function will merge many designations, from community manager to events planner.

With greater reach comes greater power but also augmented responsibility—to think ahead for your client, for your brand, and to predict how narratives change along with societal shifts. Have you heard of 'cultural appropriation', 'wokeness', and 'cancel culture'? Do you know how to deal with each of these? That's the new lexicon. A publicist today needs to work harder to stay aware of industry shifts and societal interests and be very mindful of circumstances.

Finally, the one thing that we have learnt from the pandemic is that the brands that shine are the ones who maintain a voice close to their DNA and a narrative that remains sensitive to context while staying authentic.

What takes time and persistence is to build a voice that is entirely your own, and, at the same time, sensitive to the zeitgeist. Today's consumer is very discerning and takes a holistic view of brands.

As all of our clients become content generators, what a third-party endorsement means is increasingly shifting. Ultimately, as a brand or entrepreneur, you will be your own channel, and your biggest champion. Anyone else's review, support, or dismissal comes second. In the midst of this, PR is already merging with the roles of marketing and, to some extent, sales. (I've spoken about this in 'Roots and Wings'.) We mean business in every sense now, and there's no looking back.

That said, I still get a thrill when we see a story about a client in a glossy, or when we're just about to open the doors to an event. Working behind the scenes with clients to piece their brand story together and introduce it to the world is always a privilege. We've been lucky, at Peepul, to have clients work with us for years and sometimes even a decade. Going on a brand's journey as a part of it is an indescribable experience and one I am not ready to give up just yet. It's been a roller coaster ride, and every passionate publicist lives for that adrenaline rush, the butterflies at a launch or the flutter before a story gets published. Some things never change and never should.

THE PITCH PERFECT
Playbook

Even when the idea for this book was just a thought in my head, I knew that I did not want it to be filled just with my voice, opinions, and experience. As a people person and a publicist, I know the power of community and of conversation. We do best when we work in tandem with the people around us and when there is generous give and take between everyone. So, this last section of the book is filled with expert tips, opinions, and experience. The purpose of this is to give you a resource that can answer any question you have and help you navigate anything that might come up for you in the vast, never-ending journey of branding, entrepreneurship, and communication. Putting this together was a joy because it allowed me to reach out to people who have been part of my journey at various stages, and their enthusiasm for it was very heartening.

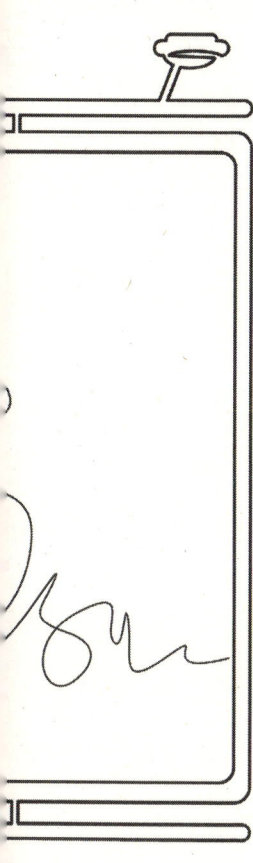

THE PITCH PERFECT

Playbook

Anita Lal

Good Earth is a brand that is, at once, Indian at its heart and global in its spirit. And the powerhouse behind it is Anita Lal. Knowing her and working with her and her fabulous team is a privilege. She has created a brand that has a strong identity, clear voice, and a seamless brand experience.

Good Earth has grown organically, and right from the start I wanted to create products that are relevant to our cultural milieu.

'*Van vaibhav*' is an important concept in Indian tradition. It means the 'splendour of the forest'. There are innumerable shlokas celebrating the splendour of the sun, the moon, the stars, birds, animals, and the forest. We humans are a part of this natural splendour and we are lost when we move away from it.

Almost all our designs are based on bringing some elements of nature into our lives—be it in actual form of birds, trees, flowers, or just with the vibrant or earthy colours of nature or the scents and oils of real flowers, resins, and grasses from the earth. We stay close to nature in Good Earth.

In India, we understand and name colours by how they appear in nature—*dhani, jamun, neel, phalsa, kairi, aasmani, geru, mayuri, pyazi, gulabi*. And this is a wonderful inspiration to celebrate the colours of the natural world around us.

Our design team has grown and evolved along with me, and by now we share the same aesthetics and values. I oversee every design and product that goes on the floor, and this results in the cohesive visual language you perceive. My natural impulse was to celebrate my love of nature, as our very name Good Earth implies.

Nearly ten years after we opened our first 1800 sq. ft. boutique in Mumbai's Kemps Corner, we moved to a to a high-ceilinged 18,000 sq. ft. store in Raghuvanshi Mills. And once again, when we had to close our Ambawatta store in Mehrauli, we then opened our shop in Khan Market. Both these moves changed our profile and moved us towards luxury with an increased customer base, and what we learnt was the importance of location.

Over the years, we have created a collaborative culture with strong ownership at every level. People [in the company] are empowered, and they identify with the brand and its values, often even more than myself. Our social media team is extremely passionate and charged and have worked very creatively even during lockdown. Even though I give my views from time to time, they have full creative space, and I am pleasantly surprised with how much they plan and achieve.

One important reason is that today our entire team is totally aligned— business, operations, marketing, and retail work in a very supportive manner despite occasional pulls and pushes and hiccups, which are inevitable. However, there is a genuine trust factor between each department and each one is committed to the common goal of brand-building.

I would tell any young entrepreneur to follow their passion, clearly define who is their target audience, and what are the values they will bring to their brand and, consequently, their customers.

Anu Duggal

I met Anu when I first moved to New York and we became part of a group of friends, which included Reshma Saujani, who you will meet a bit later in this chapter. The founding partner of Female Founders Fund, Anu is now a powerhouse in her industry for her unrelenting support of creative and innovative female-led brands. I have watched her build this career, and could not be prouder.

Women can often feel very intimidated by the idea of approaching an investor and going through that process. What advice would you give a woman entrepreneur about taking a chance on themselves and working with investors?

Develop a network of other female founders who you can lean on for introductions, pitch practice and general support throughout the fundraising journey.

What do you look for in a brand, which interests you and wants you to invest in them?

As a seed fund, we are investing primarily in people. We are looking to understand what is the unique insight/experience that you as a founder have that positions you to be successful. We also look at TAM (total addressable market) and early signs of traction. In the case of direct-to-consumer brands, we look at their social media presence to understand how engaged their followers are with their content.

If an entrepreneur were looking to scale up their business, what should they be mindful of, and how would you advise them to navigate that?

We invest only in high-growth businesses with a vision to reach $100M in revenue over a five-year period. One of the biggest challenges we are seeing is an algorithm change in channels like Facebook/Instagram has led to inefficiencies in paid spend. As an entrepreneur you need to make sure you are able to find an efficient channel for user acquisition/growth that will sustain your business for at least a two to three-year period.

What are the most common mistakes you see people making when it comes to funding and handling finances?

We often find that founders don't realize that fundraising is a fulltime job and as CEO it is part of your work even when you are not in market. It is very important to continue to take investors meetings even when you're not actively looking to raise capital. We advise our founders to always have at least nine to twelve months of runway in the bank before going out to raise additional funding, and we often find that when they let that slip to 6 months it can be difficult to attract investors.

Finally, when you engage with a publicist or PR agency, what do you look for from them, at a time when both the media and publicity are changing drastically as industries?

We've had an excellent experience with our PR firm after working with several others in the market. My biggest piece of advice when working with a new firm is to make sure that the account lead is passionate about your company. It is incredibly hard to pitch/sell a story successfully if you are not excited about the actual business itself. Finding that right fit can make a huge difference in the outcome of your PR experience.

Archana Jain

A front-runner in the PR & lifestyle space, Archana Jain is the founder and managing director of PR Pundit. With three decades of experience, Archana is one of the most respected thought leaders in brand communications and leads many discussions in improving best practices in our industry.

'No one knows what a post-COVID-19 world might look like, but what companies, brands and institutions have done to support jobs, communities and societies in rebounding successfully, will be with us for quite some time. The time has come to make capitalism better. Companies, brands and institutions must connect with their communities through authentic human acts. We have to put a human face on brand campaigns that leverage cultural flashpoints to form an emotional connection with consumers. PR will have to guide organisations to exhibit authenticity, help articulate and manifest the purpose of the organisations as an extension of their values, and then communicate this to both internal and external audiences.

While we have always communicated our client's proposition through messaging powered by trends and insights to shape brand journeys, the time has come to write a new communication playbook balanced between profit, people, and the planet. Brands are going to be left behind if they don't demonstrate true purpose. Public relations will have to work with institutions to bring-to-life changes that will have deeper impact on its stakeholders. An organization's success is no longer being measured by its bottom-line alone but what matter is its triple bottom line: financial performance, social performance, and environmental performance! It is an opportunity for companies to take action that matters — to help solve real societal challenges.

We are also living in times of predictive analysis, therefore real-time monitoring of trends, consumer touchpoints through social listening and other means is key. Measurement and interpretation of results has become indispensable. We are required to incorporate more data into reporting to provide clear evidence of value.'

Dilip Kapur

Dilip Kapur, the founder of Hidesign, trained my lens on branding in India, from design codes to consumer behaviour. One of my most memorable meetings with him was actually our first lunch, sitting in the heart of his factory, by a pond with ducks sauntering around. So try and imagine this conversation in that setting!

Often brands find it hard to identify their target audience. Hidesign has been brilliant at not only doing that but also constantly adapting to that customer's needs. Could you talk us through how you have mastered this and built it into your business?

We've always believed that our target audience has been the same across the world—a young, modern, cosmopolitan customer who is very strongly career oriented and for whom travel is part of their normal life.

We feel this lifestyle is similar across the world with those who are successful with their careers. We haven't changed very much over the years, we have also consistently kept the same values that we had right from the beginning in terms of sustainability and craftsmanship and innovation.

We've never copied a brand abroad; we've stayed true to what Hidesign was. This has made things very easy to attract a customer base that has stayed loyal to us, because the integrity of our innovation and our belief in sustainability comes right from the beginning.

The media landscape has now completely changed, and digital/social media is very influential. As a company, how do you approach the balance between traditional and social media? Do you see one being more influential or important than the other?

The media landscape can change, but as far as we're concerned, what we're interested in is to be present and communicate wherever our consumer is spending their time. Our number one priority has consistently stayed the same—our own stores. We've always felt it's not the media but the experience that our customer has of the brand at the store that is most critical. The media is an intermediary that helps us to reach large numbers of people, and that continues to be valid even in the traditional media but now increasingly digitally.

It's just that digital social media allows us to directly be in touch with our customer base and the customer that we want to contact. Being directly in touch is a huge advantage that we have now, and the numbers are far more interesting, with more than a million followers on social media and more than 3,00,000 unique visitors on our website every month, it's extremely important that they get the experience we provide them. The communication we provide them is as good as we ever did before.

What makes the Indian retail market interesting?

The most interesting thing about the Indian retail market is that it's one of the fastest growing in the world. Secondly, as a large country with a very strong culture, new brands like Hidesign have an opportunity to create their own space without being crushed by existing brands that come into the country.

This would be very unlike the smaller markets in South East Asia for example, or the Middle East, where the international brands are just so large and the cultural influence from the countries where these brands come is so powerful that local brands have had very little opportunity

In a competitive market, how does one build a lasting legacy? Hidesign is now an iconic brand that stands very clearly for its values. How have you achieved that?

We believe getting an opportunity to create a brand in the Indian market enables us to get strength sufficiently to be an international brand, which is critical if the brand is to be successful. I think being consistent has been the most important strength that Hidesign has had. Since we are not looking at trends and copying other brand trends, we've always had our own story to continually build on. I think this is what the late Yves Carcelle of LVMH taught me when we discussed brand-building. It seems difficult, because it's far easier to see what is happening internationally and replicate that in the Indian market. Building on your own brand however is like stacking brick after brick until you have a building that stands strongly on its own.

Divia Thani

Global Editorial Director for Condé Nast Traveler, *Divia Thani's track record has been wonderful to follow. Building on a career in lifestyle media in India, she has been soaring with increasingly powerful roles in the traditional media space.*

What makes a brand's storytelling compelling?

Storytelling is at the heart of the human experience. It's what makes connections amongst people. Brands get it right when they widen the scope of their stories, when they don't underestimate the intelligence of their audiences. When they go too narrow—people must convey a singular message, must look a certain way, live a certain lifestyle—that's when the story falls flat. It feels inauthentic even when it's true.

Let's shift the function of storytelling to a different context. Given your new role as Global Editor of *Condé Nast Traveler* and the fact that you have led a magazine through the COVID-19 pandemic, how would you describe the evolution of telling stories in today's reality?

During the pandemic, when travel was completely on pause, *Condé Nast Traveler* saw more than a 100 percent growth in digital traffic. At a time when travel was taken away from us, we realised the importance and value of travel in our lives. We became obsessed with travel. Overall, the pandemic has made all of us re-evaluate our priorities, and we know that people and experiences matter more to us than any products can.

So the rise in interest in travel, in being able to spend time with people we love, out in nature, safely and comfortably, is at an all-time high. The return to travel is going to be gradual in some ways and a huge rush in others. For CNT, this is an unprecedented opportunity. We are an established authority on travel, and our audience trusts us. So our role is to hand-hold them through this return to travel, guide them through all the uncertainty and questions they have, and provide truly reliable, honest information they can use in addition to inspiring them with the most compelling content across every platform they connect with, whether print, digital, social, video, or events.

Separately, we are strong partners to the travel industry, and spent 2020 doing everything we possibly could to support them during the most challenging time they have faced. In fact, some of the content I am most proud of was created during the pandemic.

For instance, Under One Sky, which was the first global collaboration amongst all CNT editions across the world, happened organically and was a testament to the fact that we were all truly united in our experiences for a brief moment in time. And *Borders Closed, Hearts Open*, which is a video showcasing the incredible work that the hospitality industry across India was doing during the worst of the pandemic, feeding thousands of people, hosting frontline workers, etc. It made me so proud to be a part of this industry. The stories we tell have to reflect the realities of our time, keeping our values intact.

How would you describe PR's role and relevance in this day and age?
PR today is a 24/7 job and must be viewed more holistically. There is still a great divide between traditional PR agencies and digital marketing agencies. Too many brand accounts are boring and drab with zero engagement. Too many agency heads look at a number of followers and likes and have zero idea what that actually means or does not mean. They don't have the ability to interpret or analyse or determine the authenticity of what they see online.

The business needs to expand its horizons and truly understand that communication today must go across platforms to wherever all your stakeholders are. They're not going to change their reading habits to come to you and digest what you want them to see in the daily newspaper. You need to be able to communicate your message and tailor it for each audience and platform, keeping your brand values in place.

Your PR strategy is no different to your overall growth strategy. If you're dealing with a publicist who isn't sitting in on your business strategy meetings, fire them. You've got to make it a larger part of marketing, and therefore you must see tangible ROI. Brand-building is part of that. Don't get swept away by people saying, 'Everyone is now on TikTok'. Or, 'We have to get on Clubhouse'. Where is your audience? What are they consuming? What do they care about? What do they need? That's what you have to address. Be platform agnostic. A new app is not a strategy. Your content, your storytelling is the strategy.

Finally, what would your checklist be for brands when it comes to building better relationships with the media?

1.   Do your research! Tell me why this should matter to me.
2.   Customise every pitch you send out.
3.   Update your databases continuously.
4.   Follow all your contacts on their social media channels.
5.   Never call without sending an email first; then wait twenty-four hours.
6.   Say thank you when you find a piece about your brand in the press. It's amazing how many calls I get saying 'please' but how few thanking us.
7.   Build relationships with different people at the media house. Don't rely on the editor alone.
8.   Spell check all your communication.
9.   If you're asking for a call or meeting, have your notes/points ready. Don't waste your time or mine.

Fern Mallis

I met Fern in New York, where she is considered a powerhouse in the business of fashion, and she has been a great mentor, sounding board, and champion of mine. She's been a witness to Peepul's growth, and I turn to her often for her wisdom and advice.

What makes a fashion brand successful? In all of the time you've spent working in the business, has there been a common thread among the brands and individuals who stay the course?

For a fashion brand to be successful, it needs a vision that is clearly communicated and a product that differentiates itself from other products on the market. Consistency is important over time for a consumer to be able to depend on a brand.

What is the first piece of advice you would give a young entrepreneur who wants to launch a fashion or lifestyle brand?

Having proper financing at the start is imperative. Whatever amount of money you think you need, triple it. Engage with a lawyer at the very beginning to have all your documents, branding, logos, etc. in place before you need them. Surround yourself with people you trust who have your back and are smarter than you. Advice is free from too many people.

As a fashion business grows, diversifies and/or pivots, how can the founder/top team make sure they continue to align with their core values?

It's important for the top-tier management to understand its core consumer, and you must prioritize investing in them and continually stay in touch with them.

The consumer today is very different from who she/he was even a year ago. What would your advice be to the fashion world at this point? How can brands and individuals continue to engage with their customers?

To engage with customers these days, you have to understand the value of loyalty. It's more economical to service and cherish your existing customers than it is to try and gain new ones. Engage in storytelling on all the platforms they are on—be it Instagram, Facebook, Twitter, TikTok, or others. You can't just depend on your website because e-commerce is now available on every platform.

Be creative in order to keep their attention, and be a brand with purpose and a mission. Consumers reward brands that stand for something they believe in, from saving the planet to saving society or curing cancer. This can be more important than presenting or following the latest trend.

You have spent decades shaping and observing the fashion industry, both in the US and all over the world. Do you see COVID-19 and the fallout of this pandemic as a defining moment for the industry?

COVID-19 and this global pandemic is a watershed moment for everyone and every industry in every corner and country in this world. It has been a time of reflection and reinvention which will continue for years to come. The fashion industry has suffered crushing blows, with stores and designers who have gone out of business, while the luxury sector has made record profits—all an indication of the bigger problems the world has to solve.

Whether through bankruptcy or merger and acquisition, this climate provides the opportunity or the impetus to build a better, smarter business; digital first, less stores, less inventory, new calendars, better timing, and better-made and sustainable products.

If we get specific about the Indian fashion business, what do you think makes it interesting? What is the industry getting right and what is it getting wrong?

The Indian fashion industry has always been fascinating to me. There is great talent here, and the colours, patterns, prints, and embellishments are unrivalled. Yet Indian designers have yet to break through in a meaningful way around the world. This I still believe is their personal choice to not do the heavy lifting that is required to become a world-known brand. This is okay, because the domestic Indian market is big enough to satisfy them, but I'm frustrated that the rest of the world is deprived of their talent. But as this world continues to evolve and globalize perhaps this can still change.

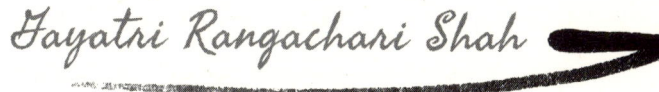

A prolific columnist and a published author, I have always admired Gayatri's effortless ability to straddle many beats in the luxury space, from art to fashion.

'Who, what, where, when and why? For me, these simple five words are the guiding principles in pitching stories. Editors are a harried lot, inundated by emails, calls and meetings. How, then, do you attract their attention and hope for a positive response? By honing a pitch so finely that they feel compelled to reply.

That doesn't mean you should submit a two-page email – in fact, the lengthier the email, the more likely that they will be to skim and skip over it. Keep it brief and to the point!

What is the story you want to tell? Sum this up in a sentence or two at the most.

Who do you want to tell it to? Is the publication or editor you are pitching to the right one for this story? Will their audience be *interested* in the story you want to tell?

Where and **when** did the story occur? Is it "newsy" and timely? Will the readership/viewership want to know more?

Why should anyone care about this story?

Only once you've answered these fundamental questions in your head should you sit down to write the pitch.

The first ever freelance story I wrote for The New York Times was about an Indian art collector. No one had ever heard of him. He had never been interviewed or appeared in the press. Yet he had a fabulous modern Indian art collection. Why would Times' readers care about such a guy? Well, for one, he was on the board of a well-known American museum. Two, he was considering bequeathing his collection to this institution. There was an 'angle' and it was newsy—after all, when do you ever hear of an Indian donating their art collection to an American museum? That's how I crafted my pitch. Yes, it got picked up. After that one article, I went on to freelance regularly for the paper across different sections.

In the example I provided above, I knew that mine was an original story. But it's important to always check to see if a publication or organization has covered the topic you are pitching and if so, what are those past stories and will your pitch add something new or different to the subject? Research your topic enough to be knowledgeable about it. Also, please don't pitch story ideas in which you have a vested interest—like a new brand that belongs to your cousin or an artist whom you grew up with. Conflict of interest is a real cause for concern in today's media landscape and editors do not want to be caught unaware.

In sum, answer the questions – why would anyone care about this story and why is it important to tell this story – before writing your pitch. And remember, be concise and write well!'

Hemant Sagar

Hemant and I know have now known each other over a decade, and I still can't help breaking into French in a conversation with him or expect a joke to be cracked at the most serious meetings. With a cutting-edge factory in Noida, Hemant Sagar and Didier Lecoanet have had the most unconventional journey from Paris to Delhi, with their label Lecoanet Hemant. They have built a stellar skillset from haute couture to easy fashion, and I always admired them for being true visionaries.

'When I was fifteen, I visited a couture shop run in Germany by the mother of a classmate. This was in the early 1970s, and she was making very classical, simple clothes. When I entered the workshop, it felt like coming home to a monastery I did not know I belonged to. And I have retained that sense in me, still, about fashion and making clothes. So we have worked to build a small Indian brand at an international level, rather than a big shiny brand for the domestic market.

India doesn't have the means to train fashion professionals at all levels, we have no pattern makers, for instance. But the marvel of India are the hands of our artisans and craftspeople. They contribute to the success of so many international and domestic brands. And this is a great asset.

The truth is that fashion has no real mainstream—it's a business of niches. You cannot compare H&M and Zara, or Tarun Tahiliani and JJ Valaya, or Comme des Garçons and Chanel. And there is nothing revolutionary about the daily act of wearing clothes or the idea of fashion. It's what you do with it with your brand. Fashion is not about creating pieces for one person, it has to be about the multiple.

I decided that if I have to make clothes that make women beautiful, I had to be more practical, and so we shifted to daily clothes and not occasion wear. I didn't want to enhance a family, I wanted to enhance a woman, so we don't do bridal. We stuck to European principles of dressmaking and have always wanted to showcase our own handwriting. And that's how we built a niche for ourselves that is now paying off.

We have always stuck by our principles, vision, and aesthetics. I feel very strongly about my vision, but we've reshuffled it and approached it on different levels when necessary. For example, I feel that there is more to the world than synthetics, so the fabrics we use complement our vision and love for nature. While people might think that Ayurganic (our range in which we work with fabrics that are infused with herbs, in an ancient Ayurvedic technique) is disruptive, our final products are also practical.

Manish Malhotra

Does he need any introduction? Manish Malhotra is a force in fashion, costume design and perhaps the most sought-after celebrity brand name in bridal design. He has become a dear friend as we worked together for several years—I am always pleasantly surprised by his childlike enthusiasm about every new trend or every new challenge, a spirit that drives his unstoppable energy and certainly boosts his teams and partners.

'Lessons and learnings are part of every day, and as a person, I never dwell upon the past. I also tend to look at the positive side of things, which immensely helps dial down the unnerving pressure and anxiety of running a business as an entrepreneur.

When I got into retail, the competition was much less, and hence, it was controlled and monopolized. As we have progressed with the times, we have become more defined and organized in service, experience, and the overall landscape. Personally speaking, I love this space. The present system allows a fair opportunity for everyone. Today, anyone can open a store or sell things online. It's much easier now. Back then, it wasn't so easy.

I remember reaching out to the big retailers with my sample outfits to introduce my work then; it was quite a journey. I want to look back and celebrate many moments, it needn't be just those prestigious awards or acclaims, but a simple acknowledgment of your work is something one should celebrate, at least I do. For me, the milestone moment in my label was when I took two sample outfits to retailers, and I got a call from them the same day to make more pieces as they were sold in just a few hours. When your design resonates with the audience, you know you're on the right track.

Like it or loathe it, social media has become indispensable to brands across formats, across industries, and fashion is no different. Especially when the pandemic struck [in 2020], our digital dependence skyrocketed, and it's unlikely that the trend will shift from here, anytime soon. At Manish Malhotra, we treat our brand pages with dedication. We ensure we give our customers a seamless experience through the world of Manish Malhotra. We not only present our imagery and aesthetics, but our values, including a peek into our customer service, quality and we present together a wholesome story of our network and our innovations in the domain. During the pandemic, we even launched India's first designer virtual store where consumers from all around the world could visit the Manish Malhotra store digitally, look around, shop and even book personal online consultations with the team to help them put together their look. This worked really well.

In total, the brand has five official Instagram accounts, including my personal one and have amassed over 11 million followers integrated. There is a separate in-house team to handle these pages' daily operations that span from generating assets, copywriting, scheduling, and marketing. Overall, it's an important domain for our brand.

Customer relations just boils down to being authentic. However different the audience is, your brand language can't vary. Having said that, I do stand for 'collaborative aesthetics,' and we take pride in our hyper-personalization. Designs may vary as per the brief, but our overall work quality, aesthetics, finishing, customer service, post-purchase service, pricing, etc., are always standardized and is something that is religiously followed. The same is maintained and communicated on our social media as well. We ensure to keep the brand language intact across platforms, and the rest is automatically taken care of.

My journey in the fashion space is quite unique. I started as a costume designer and then ventured into retail, so I built my relationships within the industry by working in Bollywood. From here on, when I started my label, a lot of celebrities who attended my fashion shows in the capacity of my friends were seen as a marketing move from the brand, which wasn't right. I remember having Urmila Matondkar as a showstopper in my first show because we were friends from *Rangeela*, and it holds the same for every Bollywood celebrity.

Many times, a celebrity adds a personality to your label. My first idea is to understand the semblance of the association, in a way, if it fits the celebrity personality. The Manish Malhotra label is always associated with Bollywood, partly because of my journey from the film fashion space and partly because of the trust the brand has won over the years. It might seem easier to navigate through this crowded space with the who's who of Bollywood wearing your creations, but what people tend to forget is the hard work that goes behind it. Decades of relentless hard work and consistent quality when you're a trusted enterprise in this space means there is zero scope of errors and spot-on delivery every time. So, I would say the pressure is always equivalent to the trust and fame that comes with Bollywood.

The Indian retail and fashion landscape are much more organized now, and it's only getting better over and onwards. The international marketplace has become smaller than ever with the advent of social media, where you are competing with brands in your home country and the one's sitting abroad. This means we've to keep strategizing on the retail front, visual merchandising, focal décor, use of technology & customer service. Thankfully the response online has also been encouraging so far.

There is a clear distinction across all the formats and spaces of couture, pret, bridal, exclusive, multi-brands and in-house brand. Various outlets cater to specific market needs, and all that has made the market much more streamlined. Above all, there is a vast network of manufacturers and retailers online who are just a click away.

Overall, I feel that the scope and opportunity to buy, sell, interact, and engage within the network and reach to the consumers have dramatically increased in the present format. As this interconnectedness strengthens, we are, in fact, launching into a much more robust business environment.

Growing a fashion brand is, to me, about honesty, sincerity, and the willingness to give those 24 hours of commitment. On the brink of starting my label, I was offered a film to direct, but I must confess I sacrificed that for my brand. It's vital to prioritise what's important at that point. Today after 31 years of establishing the label, I am now ready to venture into directing my first film. Everything happens at the right time. When you start something, you're also experimenting, but eventually, you've to find your genre and your true calling. For me, that was the bridal couture space at the time. Also, it's about consistent learning and evolving. Keeping abreast with times and keeping pace with them is of utmost importance for any growth.

At times, I felt alone, very alone because of no support or critique, but my idea of having a showstopper and celebrity donning designer attires is a norm today, which was started by me. I was bashed for it, but then, today, I get to have the last laugh when everyone, literally everyone, runs behind the celebrity with their outfits. For me, it was, in fact, a very organic process because I came from the movies, I had my relationship with these actors, and they are my friends. So, calling them at my fashion show wasn't any strategic move, back then and even now.

If I were to chat with someone who wants to start a fashion label, I would advise them to stay true to their design language and philosophy. Basically, you stick to your guns even if the world says otherwise. I never dwell on someone else's business. My greatest virtue could be minding my own business. I've always focused on my journey and my career, which has helped me cut through the confusion and stay relevant over these years. Finally, it's heart and hard work, and then, the economics follow.'

Namrata Zakaria

To me Namrata is a truly unique voice in Indian fashion; her reviews and reportage are backed by experience and strong opinions. When she was a columnist at Mumbai Mirror, *we would read her column first every morning. Partly, it was because we were excited to see what she had to say but also often fearful to find out something about a client she may have heard before we did.*

What are the attributes of a successful brand, in your experience and opinion?

It's amazing how the definition of a successful brand has evolved over the years. At one time, it was simply considered to be successful if it made a decent profit.

If you ask many CEOs today, they will insist that a successful brand is one with a fat bottom-line, and perhaps an uptick curve. But today, especially with the advent of digital and social media, we know that 'marketing' is as important as 'product' in a successful company. A brand that is constantly engaging with its consumer is vital to its recall and building loyalty. Ironically, consumers are looking for better communication. Social media is the new shop girl, and it needs to be fussing and fawning over the consumer constantly.

I also think that brands that invest in human capital are always better received. How happy are your employees? How clean is your back office?

How maximum are your minimum wages? These are vital questions that consumers ask these days. Healthy companies are those that invest inwards too, in health, education, development of skills, reforms, and equitable culture of their employees and their immediate environment. Nike, one of the most 'successful' companies in the world, and one that invests hugely in marketing itself as a political reformer especially with its constant call for racial equality, is facing a mammoth professional crisis thanks to its toxic work culture.

Storytelling is now an essential part of brand-building and marketing. What do you think brands get right when it comes to this aspect? And what are the most common mistakes or missteps you see brands making?
No one gets it right all of the time. Somebody like Sabyasachi, whose luxury label the entire fashion industry watches and apes, has made mistakes too. Brands, and companies, are allowed to make mistakes. It's important to acknowledge them. This only adds to the brand's persona and makes it more relatable. Story-telling is a much bandied about word these days. But it is something that brands must seek within themselves. You cannot do what your competition does, it needs to be your company's back-story, ethos, struggles, and successes.

Each company, and its founder, needs to find its own narrative. Develop it slowly and tell the same story in many different ways for several years. Story-telling must also evolve with the times, and must be strong enough to buttress the resistance. Case in point, the fabulous Tanishq campaigns: they have often shown advertisements discussing remarriages or inter-caste marriage and are a wonderful representation of modern India. On the other hand, I find that Zoya, also by the Tata group, struggles with a lack of image or perspective.

What would you tell brands about building relationships with the media?

1. With media, there is a fine balance to be maintained. There mustn't be too much interaction, and there mustn't be too little either.

2. Different media offices, and persons, serve different roles. Brands need to know how to pitch a story to whom. While it may not work for one media company/ person, another may lap it up.

3. Media persons, even the good ones, are quite spoilt and need a lot of assistance in doing their job. More so as they work against crazy deadlines. Promptness, efficiency, clarity of communication are par for the course. Never let a media person's phone call go unanswered, however bad the controversy.

4. Know that just because you advertise with a media company, doesn't mean you will always get favourable press. Not in the better media companies for sure.

5. I find that honesty is always the best policy in any relationship, personal or professional. If your product is good, and your marketing ethical, you will find your space editorially.

How would you describe PR's role and relevance in today's day and age?

Public relations is moot for any business. Never mind the changing media-scape, public relations will exist as long as companies exist. The PR office's job isn't just staying in touch with the appropriate press and disbursing news, but it is also teaching companies how to communicate better, whether externally or internally. Several PR firms also double up as brand strategists, which is excellent as they constantly ideate in creating news to disburse as well. As a journalist, much of my job is made easier with the assistant of PR teams. Not only do they give you verified information, they are prompt and do a lot of leg-work for the journalist as well.

Payal Singhal

I have known Payal—who heads up her eponymous fashion label—for nearly two decades, and I like to call her my lucky charm (while she likes to call me a broken record). Payal signed our first contract in New York and then in Mumbai, back in New York for my short stint—we have been in each other's businesses beyond our collaborations. Watching Payal soar internationally and in India while charting her own rules and carrying everyone in her success makes me always look up to her as an entrepreneur and a close friend.

'When I started my label in 1999, the Indian fashion industry was very young. There were only a handful of designers and boutiques, and the opportunity for publicity and public relations was so limited. I remember there were just a few fashion magazines—getting a centrespread in Femina was the only goal. Newspapers did not always have sections that covered the industry and we had no fashion weeks. In these twenty-one years, I have seen the industry go from having a very limited footprint to becoming a force to reckon with.

Now, we have hundreds of designers launching brands; we have two major fashion weeks; international magazines are here; and social media, influencers, and stylists are vital players. It is a proper industry now. For a brand to stay relevant and keep going for years, it is important to be able to adapt and pivot with the changing times. You've got to be able to put your head down, work hard, absorb every influence around you, and keep learning. Remember that as a designer, you are not bigger than the brand.

Social media and the mainstream media now coexist, and I think it is important to strike a balance. There is a permanence to the mainstream media—something about the written word gives it heft and validation. Social media can sometimes seem more transient and lighter in spirit because it's here today and gone tomorrow. So I really believe in working on relationships and publicity holistically—from social media to mainstream media to your communication with your actual customer and the experience you offer at your stores. It all has to tie in with your branding, brand language, and marketing.

I think PR plays an extremely important part in the brand's journey because it sets the tone for the brand language and its relationships with the media, with consumers. It helps you shape your company's journey and is a very important pillar of business. Like every industry, PR needs to pivot, evolve, and stay engaged with every medium and platform.'

Preeta Sukhtankar

Meeting Preeta is better than an expresso shot. Just as she always generously shares tips and her experience, here she explains the power of consumer first. She is the founder of The Label Life, an online fashion and lifestyle store that stocks elevated essentials.

Can you talk about your journey with The Label Life? When you started it, social media was not the explosion that it is today. Along the way, how have you seen the role of Instagram, influencers, and celebrity culture shape your brand?

From the time I started The Label Life, what's remained constant is having a direct relationship with our customer. What's changed is the format in which we have done this. Earlier, we relied heavily on pop-up events, for example, to allow our customers to browse our products and reach out to new audiences. Our celebrity stylists [Malaika Arora, Suzanne Khan, and Bipasha Basu] brought a sense of credibility and value at the time that was exclusive to The Label Life as we were one of the first brands to pioneer this model. We had always started out as a digital-first business, and with the growth of social media, that only fit our model better and allowed us to seamlessly integrate both online sales and strengthen customer relationships.

Today we use social media both as a broadcast and as a listening tool to really listen to what our customers want and deliver on those demands faster than we did before. We see our customers as our strongest influencers, to be honest, and love sharing snapshots of them in our products because of the power in peer reviews and feedback more than any other influencer-led strategy.

How do you handle your PR without an agency?

We think of PR first and foremost as a conversation with our customers and not only with the media. Our tone of voice and our approach is just like you'd speak to a best friend about how to feel confident, inspired, and empowered, and accordingly we design all of our communication.

An important component of doing it in-house is ensuring that everyone who works in any department dealing with external stakeholders understands our brand identity, who we are, and what we stand for. We do conduct trainings in-house on the kind of communication we want going out from our side, but more importantly, we emphasize building a relationship with the customer, so that it's more than just a PR tool.

Handling it in-house allows greater speed of communication across teams and a higher sense of urgency to resolve any issues. We also empower all of our teams to take decisions at their level, which helps ensuring that we're always responsive to issues whenever they arise.

You have partnered with celebrities who amplify your brand but don't take over it. How do you strike that balance?

I invested significant time at the start in building trust between the celebrities and our brand. They need to trust that The Label Life is a partner to them and their needs as well and that the brand always delivers on our promises. We are very mindful of the asks we make of our celebrity stylists keeping their busy schedules in mind and always ensure that we utilize their presence in the most meaningful ways by presenting a clear picture upfront of what each engagement will be like. As a result, they see themselves as collaborators in the process and have high ownership but also high trust in us to take the best decision for the brand.

What would your advice be to women entrepreneurs? They can often feel too intimidated to handle investors and other stakeholders. How do you navigate that and what have you learnt across the years?

My biggest learning is that it's impossible to convince someone else until you yourself are 200 per cent committed to your idea and goals, and to not measure yourself by what you don't have, such as a certain set of skills or a particular type of past experience. Women are often told they are 'too ambitious', but that's exactly what is needed to make a big impact—a big, bold idea that stands out and hasn't been done before. Whenever I speak with investors or other stakeholders, I always go back to my story, of what inspired me to start this business, of the potential I see and how I plan to achieve it. These three points are often clear and simple enough to get your point across.

Where do you see e-commerce and lifestyle retail headed?

Indian e-commerce is due for a revolution. The events of the past year showed us that people are now more than ever willing to go online. A few trends that we predict will take centre stage in the coming years are the rise of subscription-based ventures, either standalone or as part of existing brand offerings, customized/personalized products, and the rise of social commerce models with an increasing focus on direct-to-customer brands.

Pooja Dhingra

If you have lived in Mumbai, you can't have missed the Le15 macaron (my favourite is pistachio). And wherever you live, you probably follow Pooja on Instagram. Her career as a chef has led to not only a beautiful entrepreneurial journey with the Le15 Patisserie brand but also led to many books that are for keeps.

'Le 15 turned eleven in 2021. When I founded it, I was a young entrepreneur and chef and definitely didn't have a plan or strategy with social media. I just knew that there had to be a way for me to tell my story. This started with my blog in 2010 and then slowly transitioned to Facebook, Instagram, Snapchat, Twitter, and now YouTube.

Storytelling for me is an inherent function and comes naturally, which I like to believe has really helped shape my work. I took to Instagram as a platform from day one and have never exited it. Very early on, I understood the power of social media and the ease with which a message can be magnified. That's helped me with everything, whether it's designing menus, brand collaborations, store launches, or even writing books.

My key pieces of advice on handling social media as an entrepreneur and for your brand are:

1. Be real and honest: People like to connect to someone they can relate to. Highlight your strengths but acknowledge your weaknesses when needed.

2. Be consistent: It's important to find a platform that works for you and then be consistent in building there.

3. Build a community: I heard this so many times and while it seems like industry jargon, I saw the true value and potential of this when we closed the cafe [in Mumbai, in 2020] and sold e-books online. We had a community of people cheering for us and helped us get back on our feet.

4. Be patient: Building anything takes time and doesn't happen overnight. It's important to be patient and persistent.

We've always been a customer-focused brand, and it's been very important to me that all our customers feel special. Having celebrities amplify our work truly helped us build Le15 and just made us known to a larger audience. We really value that and our relationships with them. The balance is very important because you don't want to alienate customers and make them feel your brand is not approachable. I ensure that our content showcases the work we do and gives equal importance to all customers.

The world of investors and fundraising is extremely intimidating and something I'm still learning how to deal with. I think the key is to know your value and what is unique to you. This is not easy, and there's so much noise around you constantly. What works for me is to keep going back to the core reason and my WHY for being in this business. The biggest lesson 2020 taught me was to go back to that reason. For us, it's always been about bringing someone joy through our products and experiences and I realised I didn't need physical cafés for that. This led me to focus on our packaged goodies and that changed the game.

There are far too many lessons I've learnt over the years. But from having navigated the pandemic, I think what I have learnt is to be open, honest, and vulnerable as a leader. I'm an Oprah Winfrey super fan, and one thing that I've learnt always works is that when you're overwhelmed or confused, the best thing you can do is just make the next right move. When faced with a challenging situation, I ask myself what's the best next thing I can do given all the information I have, and I build from there.'

Priya Tanna

The founding editor of Vogue India, *a job she held for fourteen years, Priya is possibly my closest friend in the media, and she has always been a guiding light to me. I am very grateful for her support and advice, which has helped me navigate the work culture in India, as well as understand the lifestyle space so much better.*

How would you define a successful brand?

Bottom line (pun slightly intended), it's about getting your DNA right and being able to adapt and evolve without losing sight of your core values, identity, and who you are. Who is your audience? What place do you want to have in their life? What makes you unique and compelling? It is critical to have a clear mission statement that serves as your road map. You can't be everything to everyone.

For instance, 2020 has been an unprecedented year, a year where everything changed, from the way we greet each other to the way we work. But what anchored us was a global campaign we launched across all our editions world-over earlier in January, 'Vogue Values'. It became a timely reminder of the power and resilience of *Vogue* and of *Condé Nast*. It reminded us of who we are as a brand, as a magazine, as a global force and of what really matters in very uncertain times.

How can brands get better at storytelling?

John Steinbeck once said: 'A great lasting story is about everyone, or it will not last. The strange and foreign is not interesting—only the deeply personal and familiar.' Of course, he was probably talking about the great American novel so break this down a bit. Great brand storytelling needs to be for your version of 'everyone', which would be your target audience; you need to know exactly who they are and figure out how best to communicate with them. And your messaging needs to be 'personal and familiar', which would be communicating the experience and vision of your brand. For both, you need to be authentically true to who your brand is. The brands that get it right know who they are. Brands who don't, do not. I think the most common mistakes are not understanding your brand and not consulting the right experts to help tell your story.

Most brands are now content creators, alongside their engagement with mainstream media. How can they successfully bridge both?

There is nothing wrong with brands communicating with their customers directly; in fact, I would encourage them to. Here you are communicating with existing followers, and it's a great space to build and nurture brand loyalty. But today, communication cannot be restricted to just one channel. If brands are looking to target newer audiences or a way to offer a different experience of their brand, if they need brand recognition or recall value, or are trying to contextualize their brand in the bigger market out there, they need to find the right media partners and collaborations.

Priyanka Jill

Priyanka and I met when she first moved to India, and now she is running a digital empire out of London. The founder and CEO of POPXO—Plixxo, she is also co-founder and president of MyGlamm, the homegrown beauty brand that is hugely successful and innovative.

Everyone knows it is important to be on social media and to build brand communication online, but what are the key things to remember, in a saturated space?

Being on social media is now mandatory for brands. And it is essential for you to define yourself, or others will define you in ways you may not like. It is a noisy space with everyone bombarding everyone else and every brand has to focus on how to stay competitive and speak to their customer clearly.

The key thing is to understand your objective. Not every brand should aim to go viral, for example. Certain brands can use their Instagram handle to showcase their catalogue, voice, and values. My biggest piece of advice is to never try to be everything to everyone. Instead, dive deep into why you are doing this and who are you doing this for, and then create content based on that. Finally, be consistent in your messaging to build space in the customer's mind. A great example of this is Amul, a brand that does one thing well offline.

What would you say are the basics of storytelling, on a digital platform?

Having a brand toolkit set up is the first step. Everything from your logo to the colours you use on every platform need to be chosen carefully. Set your brand tone and voice. Do you want to sound funny or snarky? Work from the customer's point of view. All communication then has to be consistent—if you start off being funny, you cannot then take a serious tone of voice, or you will damage your standing.

Understand the format for which you are writing and please don't use one piece of content everywhere. Instagram is low on words and high on visuals. For a press release or blog post, words matter more. And LinkedIn is its own game. Know your users on each platform and tailor the content accordingly.

A popular myth is that posting on social media is enough for a brand to get attention from the media and their target audience, but so much depends on the quality of storytelling. What excites you about a brand or person and makes you want to tell their story at POPxO?

We do twenty posts a day on social, so our job is to identify the good brands that we want to talk about. Personally, I look at how authentic is the brand's communication, and then I want to know if people are talking about it. Brands think it's enough to tell me about themselves, but I want to know who is talking about you because that shows me that your product is good. We also want to know what a brand's point of view is. And if you don't have one, that's a problem.

The media and PR landscapes have changed completely over the past few years but especially so in the pandemic. What do you think are the emerging trends?

The media in India is changing completely. The fact that publications are choosing to cut down on or completely shut down print editions shows the reality on the ground. What I find very surprising is how magazines are not able to translate digitally. They should have seen this coming.

Earlier, PR built a bridge between a brand and its stakeholders because media management was the only way you spoke to your customer. Even pre-COVID, all the major brands have taken control of their narrative. So the role of the publicist has been turned on its head. The lines between PR and marketing are now blurred. A brand will still want something placed in a magazine, but now a PR agency will also have to look at all aspects of brand communication and offer strategy, reach out to influencers, and look at social media. We do this in-house, but if you don't have that department, you need to hire a good agency.

As someone who has built a business from the ground up, do you have any tips or advice on how to translate your vision into a set of guidelines/a direction that a team can follow?

Every leader has her or his own style of doing things. In a start-up, the DNA of a founder gets translated into the brand and you attract people who fall in with it. Up to a certain point, the culture gets set organically. You have a level of connection with the first fifty people. I know that my early teams heard things from me, I knew their lives closely and the names of their partners and kids.

As the organisation grows, I am no longer hiring personally, and my message is no longer directly communicated to every member of the team. So there have to be consistent, codified channels of communication. Or a company's culture will get set by Chinese whispers and there can be erroneous inferences, which are best avoided.

I like to do a do a town hall once a month, in which I clearly articulate the vision and goals of the organisation. For me it is important to emphasise that POPxO is of women, by women. We are against body-shaming and we don't judge. This needs to come instinctively to everyone who works for the brand, but it is my job to put in processes and measures to make sure they know that.

Reshma Saujani

Reshma was one of my first friends in New York, and we really built a beautiful friendship. She helped me settle into the city, decoded it for me, and held my hand through all the culture shocks. A lawyer, founder of one groundbreaking nonprofit Girls Who Code, and a respected author and commentator, Reshma also introduced me to the world of politics, and I have learnt a great deal from her.

'Purpose and values are hugely important to careers and brands. Your purpose is your north star—it should guide your work, your goals, your team. Purpose and values are so important that they're inseparable.

The companies and organizations that are most successful are the ones that can align their purpose with their business goals. The two shouldn't feel like they are at odds—if and when they do feel at odds, I'd recommend that young entrepreneurs take a moment, step back, and remind themselves why they started their business in the first place. What inspired you? What communities did you set out to serve? What problem did you set out to solve?

For women who are starting their own companies, I always say to aim for bravery over perfection. Failure is okay, and not knowing everything is okay. When I started Girls Who Code, I'd never run a non-profit. But I knew that we needed to close the gender gap in tech, and I was committed to doing it.

We've known for a long time that too many of our leading companies aren't diverse, equitable, or inclusive enough—it's a part of the reason that organizations like Girls Who Code exist. This year, many companies and organizations made promises to do better. Promises are a good start, but only time will tell whether we "get it right" in the long term. I sincerely hope that we do because the future of our country, in so many ways, depends on it.

We're all responsible for building and leaving a legacy, for the community and culture we create and leave behind. To women, I'd say that legacy is ultimately about bravery. We're remembered for the chances we take, the big dreams we chase, and the failures we grow from.

I ran for office twice and failed. They were very big, very public, failures. I was devastated both times. But in the end, these failures didn't break me. To young entrepreneurs starting their careers, I would say do the brave thing and chase your dreams even though you might fail—especially if you might fail. Because once you fail, you learn that your world doesn't end and that you can keep going and keep growing.'

Shefalee Vasudev

When I moved to Delhi in 2017, I began to spend more time with Shefalee. If you read her book, The Powder Room, *which reveals the backstage of Indian fashion or her pieces on* The Voice of Fashion, *which she is the editor of, you will soon realise that her approach to brand and product is fairly counter-intuitive. It is usually from the lens of society, identity, or history—I find her writing and her voice unique in this sense as she brings gravitas to the industry.*

'For me, the most successful attribute is the quality of a product or a brand, its design as beauty and function and its relevance. A brand that blends these values becomes compelling, either because it lasts beyond a few seasons, or makes us feel a certain way or we are simply seduced by its prettiness. Resonance is key. Even brands that may not be tangible need to spark relevance in our lives. Consistency of promise and purpose matters a lot too. When a consumer spends time, curiosity, money or engagement on a brand, a relationship is seeded and for a buyer to hold on to it, it needs to be consistent. Some brands find they have fickle customers and that could well be because they do not prioritise consistency of image or the timbre of sentiment (fragrance, feeling, fascination) that the product or experience evokes. On the other hand, brands with a point of view get imprinted in recall. Can a brand find ways to ring in with the zeitgeist and yet speak for itself? Who does it invite into its world and who does it exclude? What are the ideas it communicates? These reveal its core.

I notice that designer-led brands often talk to consumers through events, social media, and a group of collaborators. This helps in forming associations, both aesthetic and visual that give us a sense of what the brand creators believe in and its culture. But if they make quick and frequent changes then the associations are lost or get muddled in recall. Of course, sponsorships and commercial collaborations influence or mandate these shifts. I don't mind if a brand always has a Bollywood star at its events for instance. Understandably, the names of these celebs would change based on whose movie is due for release or who is in the news. Yet, at least it is consistent in the broad statement that it associates with film stars.

Not all brands can tell stories well. Their ambassadors become the story or an influencer does. Often, I find myself becoming impatient with similar or repetitive stories. Ironically, photography and technology are manipulated to echo sameness instead of difference. Especially since most stories now are told digitally, technology can be used as a tool of distinction. A competent PR agency can be an enabling partner in creating a brand strategy, by building the right collaborations, selecting the right stores for retail, when and how to speak to the media, while simultaneously building a brand's social media identity.'

Sujata Assomull

I've known Sujata in her various roles in the media—she was the founding editor of Harper's Bazaar India *and continues to write for several Indian and international publications. Now, she also has a lively presence on social media, with an interest in sustainability. I love Sujata's ability to balance a brand's marketing voice with her own journalistic voice and I can tell you that this is a rare skillset.*

'It is a scary time to be a journalist, especially if you cover fashion, entertainment, and lifestyle. For a while now, everyone has been talking about how digital is now replacing all traditional forms of media, with print being the biggest victim of this phenomenon. While this is a conversation that has been taking place ever since the internet first started, the pandemic seems to have accelerated the situation, with lifestyle journalism looking like a casualty of COVID-19.

The advent of influencers had already affected the status of fashion editors. While no will ever will ever forget how fifteen years ago, in the 2006 film *The Devil Wears Prada*, Meryl Streep (who plays Miranda Priestly, a character believed to be based on *Vogue's* Anna Wintour) delivered a monologue on a cerulean blue sweater in which she says, 'It's sort of comical how you think that you've made a choice that exempts you from the fashion industry when, in fact, you're wearing the sweater that was selected for you by the people in this room." Today, this famous line, a cultural moment, delivered just one year before Vogue launched its India edition, seems outdated. Publications, especially fashion magazines, just do not hold that weight anymore.

One of the first fashion magazines to launch in India was *ELLE India*, in December 1996. It started as a bi-monthly and soon became a monthly. Though it did pause its print edition for a while during the first wave of lockdowns, it is currently a bi-monthly with a strong digital focus. Its teams were cut down but not as drastically as *Harper's Bazaar*. This magazine went on a pause too, with almost the entire team finding themselves out of work. Lifestyle journalists across newspapers too found that teams were shrinking, with some losing their jobs.

Former editor-in-chief of the magazine, Supriya Dravid, who has previously worked with *Harper's Bazaar India*, says, "With regards to fashion and features—I think one of the reasons that it got hit so badly (for the time being) was because it didn't seem to be the need of the hour given the pandemic crisis. It was about pivoting towards essential services, using social media as a tool to generate help across the board, and mustering up emotional courage to just get through the tragic state of the country." She firmly believes, however, that this is not the end of journalism but that it will just be found in new forms. "Good journalism will survive anything. If at all we learnt something as journalists, it is that COVID-19 did not kill the freedom of speech. The power of a great story is the greatest high. Journalism can never be done away with—from a punchy fifty-word edit by The Print to the poignant long format reads in The Ken, good content will always find its readers."

Interestingly, all the publications in Dravid's list are digital, and most fashion magazines in India were almost blind to the need to become digitally savvy, *Harper's Bazaar India* for instance still has no content website. It also showed that if you wanted to embrace new age mediums and be ahead of the curve traditional as a journalist, media organizations were perhaps not the right home for you.

Smart journalists will reinvent, if they want to survive, and think out of the box. Legacy titles themselves are now becoming content creators— Condé Nast India (the publishers of *Vogue*, *GQ*, *Architectural Digest*, and *Condé Nast Traveller*) made its Netflix debut with the reality show *The Big Day* on Valentine's Day 2021. And some of the best-known names in the industry are now working with e-tailers, with former editor in chief of *Elle* and *Harper's Bazaar India*, Nonita Kalra now heading editorial at Tata Cliq Luxury; Rujuta Vaidya, who worked at Condé Nast for eight years and was the co-digital editor of *Vogue India*, joining Nykaa Fashion, and Dravid, who helmed ELLE from November 2017 to June 2020, joining Ajio Luxe (part of the Reliance conglomerate) as editor in chief. So what does that mean for traditional lifestyle journalism?

Jamal Shaikh, national editor, *Brunch* and New Media Initiatives at *Hindustan Times*, has literally seen the mediascape change in front of his eyes. The former founding editor of *Men's Health*, which shut operations in 2015 in India, he started his career at *Bombay Times* in 1997, while he was still at college. One of the few young journalists who did not go dot-com in the late 1990s when that boom was a flash in the pan, he says, "Long before the word "influencer" evoked confusion, I thought of myself as one. Being a journalist didn't make you rich, it allowed you to yield influence, assess, and analyse so that your readers didn't need to think. The future of my career is going to be me continuing to be a journalist, even if you call it "content creator", "influencer", or "writer". I feel the true scope of being a journalist is just beginning to get exciting.' His own magazine, *Brunch*, went through a revamp during the year of pandemic and moved towards becoming more millennial friendly. He says, 'My biggest learning with *Brunch* catering to a millennial audience is that it is complete bulls**t that the young are shallow, have ADHD, or do not enjoy long reads. What they do not have patience for is rambling on repeat. If a point is to be made in thirty words, make it and get on with it, but if it requires 3,000 words and the subject is interesting, you can be sure the millennial reader will get to the end.'

This is a phase of transition, and those always are bumpy. Journalism may not be the force it once was but it still matters. Thirty-five-year-old Pooja Singh is national features editor and style editor of the business daily *Mint*. She says, "I started my journalism career during the 2008 recession. People discouraged me from selecting this profession, insisting print media will die soon. It's been thirteen years, and print media is still here, though not in its former shape, but it exists. I don't think print media will lose its relevance completely, at least not for another decade or so." Most editors believe that the line has blurred between journalists and content creators, yet the role of journalists within content creation is very distinct. Even when a journalist turns influencer—as some former editors have—they stand apart in the sea of content that is now available to us, as they understand how to blend truth and accuracy with opinion and have a pulse for being ahead of current trends. Says Singh, "If you need to create a niche for yourself in social media, you need to offer something unique, which comes from learning and experience. So yes, you need at least five years of experience to stand out and offer something that people can learn from."

As for the movement of journalists from media publications to corporate organizations, this is not new. Journalism (especially in India) has never been a career known for its pay, and with options being limited once you hit a senior level, leaving it was a norm for experienced journalists as they turned to corporate communications as their next career move. It is a practical move in these times. It is a transition that has been happening in the West for a while. Lucy Yeomans, the British editor in chief of *Harper's Bazaar UK*, left her position after twelve years almost a decade ago to join Net-a-Porter and launch their magazine *Porter*. She has since left the luxury e-tailer and founded her own fashion gaming app, DREST, but she started a wave. Most recently, editor in chief of US's *Allure*, Michelle has announced she is leaving her position to join Netflix as VP Editorial and Publishing.

Says Dravid of her move to Ajio Luxe, "I can only speak for myself. Having spent years of on-the-job learning, handling both the power of the written word and straddling advertisers has taught me how to mix content with commerce. At Ajio Luxe, we lean heavily on an editorial approach to a luxury e-commerce portal. As journalists, we are all content creators in our own way—this is just a refreshing extension of a new platform."

So yes, there will be a new normal for journalism. But what they will be, well, not even a crystal ball can answer that. I for one, despite having had over twenty-five years of experience in the business—having worked in newspapers, corporate communications, magazines, digital platforms, and in television—can only say throughout my career the one common thread is that everything I did was through the eye of being a journalist. That never changed. The most important role of a journalist is to respect the reader, never misinform them, to be truthful, and have a nonpartisan voice. If your audience wants things delivered in a new way, so be it. It will of course just be a survival of the fittest and most agile. But to write off journalism (and I have a vested interest here), that's wrong. The only constant in life is change. For now I am embracing being an independent journalist and am platform agnostic. And as Miranda Priestly would say, "That's all".

Tina Tahiliani Parikh

Tina is a force in the business of fashion retail in India. As executive director of Ensemble, the multi-brand chain of stores, she sets standards in the industry. We've had the pleasure of representing Ensemble, which gave me a chance to watch Tina work. A visionary who is known for her bold decisions, which she makes very quietly, she is a guide and mentor to several designers.

You have been witness to the growth of fashion retail in India. Could you talk a bit about that journey you've had with Ensemble and the industry alongside it?

When I joined the business in 1991, the industry was still in its very early days. The designers were really experimental, were developing their own style, and many pieces were like works of art. The customer too was used to going to a tailor and had to be educated on what made our pieces special, how they were more than just two meters of brocade. It was really a period of exploration, of discovery for all of us at Ensemble and the customers.

Another exciting aspect for me personally was looking at traditional Indian craft through a modern lens. For example, we worked with this wonderful designer called Asha Sarabhai in Ahmedabad. She took the traditional *kangri* and *jaali* detailing of Gujarat and reinterpreted the traditional Abha with these techniques. Or with fine block print or bandhani. It was all a very pared-down aesthetic compared to what we were used too, almost Japanese. Even Meera and Muzaffar Ali's version of chikankari was just so different than what we had grown up with in Lal Bihari Tandon.

Another significant change in my thought process was the pride I felt at what India had to offer in terms of craft, fabric, and embroideries.

We had grown up in socialist India and thought that everything cool was in America and Europe. To discover Rohit Bal's extraordinary bolero jackets painstakingly done in Kashmiri embroidery, Suneet Verma's metallic breastplate and Tarun's textured coats with latticework dupattas was mind blowing and really widened my horizons as to the possibilities that our great country, its heritage, and its creative minds could offer. I realised that we were in a very unique position. Our designers were talented but they also had this incredible backbone of craft, fabrics, and hand workmanship to base their ideas on and bring them to life. All that was needed was the right pattern and shape. This was a rare combination.

Around the mid-1990s, Indian designers discovered the big fat Indian wedding (which was relatively subdued in those days) and the power of designing bridal. This hijacked Indian fashion for a while as designers realised that bridal budgets were bigger and that those pieces were sure-shot buys instead of giving pieces on consignment to stores!

Here are what I see as key milestones to our journey

Ensemble shows. From the time of its inception till the mid-1990s, Ensemble used to host a big fashion show once a year in October, which many society women in India would attend. Fashion shows were rare in those days, and it was very exciting to discover what the new direction and trends for the year were. These shows were really the precursor of fashion weeks before they officially started in the year 2000. I used to work on these shows for at least three months of the year. Once fashion weeks started, we hosted these shows on our landmark anniversaries.

Those were the days when models really ruled the roost. There was no concept of film stars being styled or being ambassadors for brands that is so prevalent now. Mehr Jesia, Shyamolie Verma, Madhu Sapre,

Anu Ahuja, Namrata Shirodkar, Alison Kanuga, Svetlana Casper, Colleen Khan, Aishwarya Rai (before she became an actress)—these women were all supermodels in their own right. They just brought the clothes to life, and our shows were almost electric. There was an innocence and a newness to everything, from design to the shows. No one was jaded or on a commercial treadmill. There was only one show a year, and all who participated, including the audience, were excited to be there. Everyone did their best in this journey of self and industry discovery.

The contemporary phase. For me, this started with the discovery of Abraham and Thakore with their wonderful black and white ikats. At that point (1993-4), they were supplying to places like the Conran shop in London, and I had to persuade them to consider a store in India. Later I was extremely encouraged when David Abraham told me that Ensemble was as professional as the Conran Shop.

NIFT. The National Institute of Fashion Technology started a year after Ensemble. Our raison d'être has been to discover and nurture new designers. I remember such excitement at discovering JJ Vallaya and Ashish Soni in 1993. And then Rajesh Pratap in 1995, followed by Hidden Harmony, then Amrich and Péro (I think she went to NID) and a host of others like Injiri, Eka, Ikai, Bodice, and Lovebirds.

Modern glamour. Tarun's discovery of digital printing was a watershed moment in Indian fashion history, as it allowed small runs and placement printing. His Mughal t-shirts were the basis of his Milan Fashion Week collection that led to a whole new language in Indian fashion, that of India Modern, now embraced by the likes of Abhishek Sharma, Saksha and Kinni, Aseem Kapoor, etc.

The Bollywood phase. About twenty years ago, Manish Malhotra burst onto the scene, and for the first time Bollywood started impacting fashion. When Rani Mukerji wore her short kurtas and patiala salwars in *Bunty aur Babli*, this suddenly became a fashion statement. Movies like *Kabhi Khushi Kabhie Gham*, where the leading stars were dressed in designer clothes, were definitely starting to make an impact on the way people thought about clothes. The Indian fashion designers have Karan Johar to thank for making the Indian Wedding really fat, and with his influence, all the bigger players in the Indian fashion industry became seriously associated with weddings. Slowly, movie stars started impacting the common man's idea of style, and with the rise of social media about fifteen years later, this trend got cemented.

The rise of Kolkata and Hyderabad. For the first fifteen years, most of our fashion designers were based in Bombay or Delhi (Delhi slowly started becoming a bigger hub because of the craft belt and the abundance of cheaper space for workshops and *karkhanas*). About twenty years ago, designers from Kolkata started to have a serious impact on the industry. In part because of their talent, but also because of the incredible craftsmanship and pricing in Bengal. I remember flying back from a day with Anamika Khanna and just being seriously moved by the new direction her work was taking. By 2007, when Ensemble celebrated twenty years with a sit-down dinner show at the Grand Hyatt in Kalina (attended by Priyanka Chopra in preparation for her role in *Fashion*), Sabyasachi was already becoming a force in the industry. The Hyderabad designers rose to prominence about ten years ago, establishing that city as another design and fashion hub.

The textile phase. This began approximately in 2009-10. Ensemble has always been a big supporter of the sari, working directly with weavers and craftsmen. Sanjay Garg has to be credited with making textile fashionable again, followed by Payal Khandwala, Hemang Aggarwal, Akaaro, and Kshitij Jalori.

The phase of private equity. Anita Dongre was the first fashion designer to raise private equity. This was followed by a spate of investments in fashion houses by the big business groups and more rounds of private equity for Ritu Kumar etc. The industry was suddenly starting to get recognised for its potential.

The rise of online. Pernia's pop-up shop must be credited with being the first big player in this area. It's now a rising part of every designer's sales and projected to grow aggressively.

How has the Indian luxury consumer evolved over the years?
The first customers really needed to be educated on what was special about the clothes. They had to be taught to understand what made the pieces so special—the patterns, fits, cuts, and finish, and also the fact that it was an original design thought up by a creative mind. Now, the customer who is interested in fashion has a plethora of ways to be educated and has graduated to being very savvy. Of course, Instagram, Facebook, and Pinterest help.

There are those who are very influenced by Bollywood and other influencers, and then there are many who really have their own style. However, many customers, especially first-timers and brides, really need hand-holding to make the right choice. As India has become wealthier, a host of new customers have entered the arena, and for them social media is a big influence. Many of our clients are from smaller towns in India who will travel to big cities to buy the best or now shop online or from Instagram. The incredible thing about social media is that the client now has a direct connect with the designer's team.

When it comes to fashion retail strategy, what do brands get right, and what do they get terribly wrong?

I think the successful brands have had to reinvent themselves over the years, and the ones who have failed to do so have become irrelevant. So a product that keeps up with the changing times is clearly very important. However, storytelling and marketing are also crucial, and brands that have not been able to transition to do that successfully, especially since they are now able to talk directly to the consumer through social media, have suffered.

With the growth of e-commerce and social media, what do you see as the critical changes required for brands to stay relevant? How has Ensemble also pivoted to this new market?

The digital experience offered by a brand today is going to increasingly determine their offline success as well. It has to be a consistent, collaborative omnichannel experience.

Could you please share your top tips for brands who want to build a relationship with an industry leader like Ensemble?

Work on an original point of view. Quality, cut, and fit are crucial. We look for someone with a voice and someone who has the tenacity to stay committed through the years.

Vivek Sahni

I have a soft spot for maverick founders, and Vivek is a great example of one. His incredible journey has helped build a brand that is now a household name. He has an appetite for vision and scale, which speaks to Kama's growth. Personally, I want to steal every piece of art on his walls and respect how discreet and discerning he is in life and business.

'Kama Ayurveda is an Ayurvedic beauty brand that provides time-tested formulations, made with natural ingredients to the discerning consumer. What we know is that to retain a consumer we need efficacy, which means the products have to work, or people will switch to other brands. This promise of authentic and proven products that show lasting results is our key pillar, strengthening the trust and belief of a growing consumer base.

As a brand, we have always taken pride in maintaining its positioning as an authentic Ayurvedic beauty brand, using unadulterated Ayurvedic formulations to create treatments that provide lasting efficacy. These brand pillars are further strengthened with clinical claims, conducted across different products.

Our beauty treatments do not undergo any form of animal testing. We have always been very transparent with the purity of all our products. Additionally, Kama Ayurveda also has recognition and international certifications from institutions including ECOCERT, PETA and clinically-proven claims across different products that back the brand values.

I think the right investor is critical. One that shares your value systems, beliefs, etc. If they do not then you can have a disaster as you have two separate thought processes running the company. We have been incredibly lucky with both our investor sets as they have added immense value along with resecting the integrity of the brand.

As the brand started becoming a recognised name, it was increasingly important to further our information to the media with tools other than word of mouth. With a publicist stepping in, we were able to identify and maintain media hygiene, reach the right audience, via different media platforms and procure the right placements.

With the coming of a global pandemic, Kama Ayurveda, amongst other brands had to revaluate existing rules and protocols. In the wake of a complete lockdown of e-commerce and our brick and mortar stores, we studied the situation at hand, and used the time to introduce simple Ayurvedic rituals that can be practiced everyday, via our social media.

Social media has played a vital role in changing consumer behaviour and become a key platform for consumers to evaluate a brand and its offerings. Kama Ayurveda moved the majority of its communication online, with social media platforms becoming the main source of its communication. Here the brand was able to engage with consumers in the form of doctor led live sessions, facial yoga, and a broadened influencer base. Digital creators furthering the messaging of the brand, has also played a crucial role in influencing the decision making of consumers. With increased consumers switching to online modes of shopping, social media platforms have made the brands much more accessible.

As our website restarted, we endeavoured to move the majority of our communication online, and rerouted consumers to our website, as far as possible. To facilitate this, an IVR number, and online beauty consultations were some additions we made. This was also with the objective of elevating our brand experience.

When retail started to reopen, we were well-prepared, accounting for new ways our consumer would experience the brand. With the vaccine being made available, we took the responsibility of vaccinating the majority of company employees as one of the many steps towards ensuring utmost safety and precaution at our end. Constantly monitoring the journey, we ensured maintenance of social distancing, mandatory masks at all times, minimal contact, and online modes of payments, to make shopping for our products hassle-free.'

Acknowledgments

I hope that *Pitch Perfect* helps you understand my profession better and, more importantly, gives anyone the nudge in promoting a brand, or simply in learning the ropes of PR.

I have come full circle in many ways through the process of writing this book—I wanted to find a way to celebrate a few milestones for my firm, and this feels better than any party we could host. I had a chance to look back and re-connect with many friends, former colleagues and clients and reminisced on the starting point of this journey. There are many more I am grateful for who are not mentioned in the book, like the girl who helped me on my first day of employment in Paris, when I crashed my big new computer (and then continued to crash many more devices through the years).

As I mentioned earlier in the book, this profession requires as many personal skillsets as it does experience. My parents who took many years to understand what a publicist does, gave me a strong personal foundation for this job—be curious and open minded, embrace one's surroundings (whether we were in a small village or a Michelin star restaurant), and just be happy to be around people different from you. My sister Ishwari taught me the biggest lesson while she is thriving as a therapist, that success does not need to look linear. My beloved husband Sourabh has been my biggest rock and sound advisor through the years, I take my work personally and tend to dissolve into crumbs easily. He has always patiently picked up the pieces and given me the confidence I needed to make bold decisions. And I have to thank my daughter Dayani who is growing up watching me on my laptop when she isn't cuddled up next to me. She has never made me feel guilty about being distracted at many moments. I am glad that it is engrained in her that a mother can multi-task, sometimes be energetic, sometimes exhausted, and it's all okay.

When my dear friend and collaborator Chinmayee and I sealed our association with Penguin Random House India, the pandemic started with the first lockdown in March 2021. I wouldn't see my friend till nearly a year later, so this book has been a remote project for both of us, a testimony to a longstanding friendship and integrity. Many Zoom calls, voice messages and emails later, here we are. I can't thank Chinmayee enough for holding my hand through the process of writing a book which has been such a humbling journey. And we are both grateful to the best editor ever, Shreya Punj, whose tenacity and compassion have been exemplary. I have learnt so much from this gracious lady, who believed in us the moment we spoke, and I realized that, just like we work, it's all about that person who always roots for you. So Shreya, and Team Penguin India, we love you.

My career path in India has been peppered with some amazing encounters as I have hired for Peepul in various cities. In a field where turnover is an unavoidable reality, I am so proud to have built strong relations with team members who have stood the test of time.

I am so thrilled that my first marquee client, Dilip Kapur, who took a gamble by hiring me when I had just about set up in Mumbai, has shared this generous foreword.

To all of you professionals and brands who have crossed my path in the past twenty-five years, I am thankful to each one of you, as you have shaped my journey across three continents. Little did I know that I would build my own legacy in this business and be fortunate enough to document it.

The following list is to thank all the people who helped bring the book to life with their specific contributions. My gratitude goes to

Abhishek Raniwala

Anita Dongre

Anita Lal

Anu Duggal

Archana Jain

Ashiesh Shah

Ashutosh Munshi

Cecilia Morelli Parikh

Deepika Gehani

Dilip Cherian

Divia Thani

Fern Mallis

Gayatri Rangachari Shah

Hemant Sagar

James LaForce

K Radharaman

Lulu Raghavan

Malini Agarwal

Manan Gandhi

Maneka Thadani

Manish Malhotra

Mehernaaz Dhondy

Namrata Zakaria

Nonita Kalra

Pareina Thapar

Parmesh Shahani

Payal Singhal

Peter D'Ascoli

Preeta Sukhtankar

Priyanka Gill

Priya Tanna

Pooja Dhingra

Rasna Bhasin

Reshma Saujani

Dr Ruta Vyas

Sanjay Nigam

Shagun Singh

Shefalee Vasudev

Sophia Sinha

Sujata Assomull

Tarang Arora

Tarun Tahiliani

Vandana Mohan

Varun Rana

Vivek Sahni